3C© PERFORMANCE MODELING

PROVIDING THE LANGUAGE AND STRATEGY FOR SUPERIOR PERFORMANCE

TAKING ORGANIZATIONS, LEADERS AND INDIVIDUALS
TO HIGHER LEVELS OF PERFORMANCE

3C© PERFORMANCE MODELING

PROVIDING THE LANGUAGE AND STRATEGY
FOR SUPERIOR PERFORMANCE

GLENN SCHENENGA & GREGORY GAMBLE

Mill City Press
Minneapolis, MN

Copyright © 2011 by Glenn Schenenga and Gregory Gamble.

MILL CITY PRESS

Mill City Press, Inc.
212 3rd Avenue North, Suite 290
Minneapolis, MN 55401
612.455.2294
www.millcitypublishing.com

All rights reserved. No part of this publication may be reproduced, stored in a retrieval system, or transmitted, in any form or by any means, electronic, mechanical, photocopying, recording, or otherwise, without the prior written permission of the author.

ISBN-13: 978-1-937600-28-0
LCCN: 2011939611

Cover Design and Typeset by Melanie Shellito

Printed in the United States of America

CONTENTS

Acknowledgments iii

Authors' Note v

Introduction: Leading Organizational Performance —
A New Perspective vii

Chapter 1: Organizational Performance 1

Chapter 2: Defined Leadership 25

Chapter 3: Individual Performance 47

Chapter 4: Team Performance 65

Chapter 5: Mergers and Acquisitions 75

ACKNOWLEDGMENTS

Glenn and Greg have been professional consultants for over 15 years. Their mission is to help create remarkable organizations, enabling them to reach unparalleled success. Simply stated, they take organizations, teams, and individuals to higher levels of achievement and contribution. Their services are designed around the collection and use of data to pinpoint actions and strategies that will bring meaningful change and tangible improvements to clients. Knowing that no two challenges are ever the same, they offer customized solutions for maximum results.

As their practice grew, it became clear that leaders had a very clear understanding of how they needed their organizations to perform, but often that understanding was not clear to the rest of the organization. What was needed was a methodology to identify and communicate that understanding as well as a way to determine how the organization was actually performing.

Glenn and Greg teamed with David Farr, a renowned leader in organizational and leadership performance for Fortune 500 companies. David has focused his career on developing instruments and systems designed to help leaders develop the skills necessary for improved performance and personal development. David developed the 3C System of Organizational, Leadership, and Individual Performance, the proprietary system introduced in this book.

The 3C system allows leaders to clearly define how they expect their organization to operate and compares that to how the organization is really operating. It presents a simple picture of how organizations operate within three areas required for success:

1. Focused, targeted, driven, risk-taking, and goal-oriented disciplines.
2. Analytical, practical, methodical, and metric-based disciplines.
3. Interactive, relational, and collective disciplines.

Additionally, the system identifies individual performance style preferences as well as team styles, allowing individuals and leaders to properly focus on what is required to move the organization forward.

Used in Fortune 500 companies as well as small startup companies, the 3C approach has resulted in accelerated performance improvement. It is simple, fun, impactful, and easy to implement.

Our thanks go to David Farr, who has always believed that simplicity and focus are the keys to sustained performance and individual growth. His approach has yielded great results and continues to have a tremendous impact on organizations, leaders, and individuals.

www.g2ptnrs.com

AUTHORS' NOTE

3C Performance Modeling is a unique approach which has impact on organizations and teams, leaders, and, individuals. Its success lies in its simplicity. People remember it and can easily apply it. It can be used repeatedly and is always impactful.

In this book, we dedicate a separate chapter to each of the key areas of application: organizations and teams, leaders, and, individuals. We have done this so readers can go directly to the chapter which interests them. In order to ensure that each chapter can stand alone (to a degree), we have included the 3C concept descriptions in each chapter, so readers do not have to search for the concept in other areas of this book.

3C is a targeted approach to higher performance. It drives short term performance at organizations, leadership and individual levels. Our hope is that you can use the concepts outlined in this book and see how a simple, fun, energizing approach can lead to greatly improved performance.

INTRODUCTION

LEADING ORGANIZATIONAL PERFORMANCE
A NEW PERSPECTIVE

Organizations do not achieve goals by moving forward in a straight line: they "tack" back and forth, dependent on what is needed in the short term, to better attain long-term goals.

In a rapidly changing world, leadership is more challenging. Driving organizational performance requires a continued focus on the tried and true approaches of setting vision and goals, developing relationships, and then developing leadership capabilities to drive those goals.

But it now gets a little more complicated. In order to accelerate organizational performance, short-term leadership focus is also required. Long-term success (ultimately the job of leadership) requires execution on short-term deliverables. *Short-term deliverables change during the quest and require different leadership approaches from the organization.*

People in organizations need clarity and direction on what is expected of them—today, this week, this month. This critical need is often overlooked, as leadership assumes there is clarity and fails to provide it in the short term.

Driving organizational performance—both short- and long-term—is one of the central jobs of a leader and the leadership team. It is central to the success of a company. Organizational success depends, in large part, on the ability of the leader and the leadership team to clearly define the vision of a company, establish strategic goals necessary to accomplish that vision, and then ensure that the organization executes and delivers against those goals. The organization accomplishes this through "organizational alignment"—ensuring that everyone is pulling in the same direction. Many consulting firms focus on helping organizations create this alignment in their balanced scorecard process, compensation systems, training programs, and more.

There is certainly a lot of research around setting vision and goals. Most of it centers on clearly defining the vision and goals: making sure that the goals and actions of subordinate teams within the organization are properly aligned, that reward systems are appropriately designed and implemented, and that the vision and goals are repeated many times over.

A typical model for organizational success can be defined as follows:

- What
  - What is the vision—where is leadership trying to take the organization?
  - What are the leadership capabilities required to attain that vision?
  - What are the key strategic and tactical goals required to attain that vision?

- Why
  - What are the compelling reasons to do this?

- How
  - How does my department/function/team contribute?
  - How will we measure success—what are the mileposts along the way?

- How do I contribute—what is expected of me?
  - How will I be measured?
- WIFM
  - What's in it for me?

This model has proven effective and is simple in its approach. Its simplicity allows everyone in the organization to have key questions answered, and it leaves little room for ambiguity. It also forces leadership to provide clarity. Many, if not most, organizational performance models align with this in some way, and, of course, it incorporates the necessity for leadership capabilities.

There is ample research and discussion of leadership techniques and behaviors required for success. Most of this focuses on the key attributes for leadership success and the behaviors of leaders. Indeed, most successful organizations have developed key leadership dimensions and develop and evaluate current and potential leaders around those attributes; some have four or five, some have upwards of 20 or more.

The common denominators of most models include:

- Focus on the end game
- Consistent behaviors and actions
  - Define and implement the right culture
- Defined leadership attributes
  - Leadership assessment/development based on these attributes
  - Organization wide

All of these approaches have proven successful. It is not our intention to debunk these approaches. Rather, we categorically believe that setting a vision, defining clear goals around that vision, developing leadership capabilities required for success, developing those capabilities in leaders, and evaluating leadership performance around those capabilities are all foundational elements for success. Our experience consulting and working with executive leadership over the past 15 years has confirmed all of this.

However, we believe there is another dimension of leadership and organizational performance that, when coupled with the "vision/goals/capabilities" approach, actually *accelerates* organizational performance. When leaders go to the next step—namely, providing a clear picture of how they expect the organization to perform for the next two to six months and measuring the organizations success against that profile—organizational performance accelerates.

Our goal in this book is not to present a new model to drive organizational performance but rather to "add on" to the existing model. This "add on" requires leadership to retain focus on the big picture and then to develop an actual road map, or project plan, to guide the organization through a series of different performances/behaviors to get to the desired goal. By providing short-term performance and behavior clarity, the organization is better able to deliver—or identify what is blocking its ability to deliver. By ensuring that the organization—and everyone in it—knows what is expected *today* and understands that this expectation will change soon, expectations at the organizational and individual level are clarified. This allows everyone to maximize their contribution to success.

Our experience is that most organizations do not focus on short-term deliverables (which, of course, must be linked to the overall long-term goals). Additionally, we have found that almost all leaders have a very clear expectation of what they need their organization to do right now and three months from now, but that could be different from six months from now. We have seen that most leaders attempt to drive their organizations—and perhaps their leadership teams—to the behaviors and actions they (the leaders) want through sheer force of will or persuasive influence. Indeed, many leadership books and much executive coaching focuses on how to influence and drive people to the behaviors and performance a leader expects. But what the leader expects and needs today may not be what is needed two to three months from now.

So the question becomes, how does a leader continually redirect her leadership team and the organization to chart the fastest and best path to success? This is the fundamental dilemma facing leadership today. It's like sailing a boat into the wind; one must continue to tack. The skipper's job is to decide when to tack and then ensure his team is all working to change course and that they are ready, at any given time, to change course again.

Naturally, this implies that leadership capabilities and behaviors must be flexible. Leadership must be able to employ different capabilities depending on what is needed for the short-term deliverable. This is not "situational leadership," which is reactionary. This is planned, defined leadership behavior designed to drive the organization to the behaviors/performance required during this "tack."

Successful leaders:

- Have a clear understanding of actions/behaviors necessary for success
    - Short-term and long-term

- Need to keep their team focused on short-term deliverables but keep linkage to long-term goals
- Must define and drive short-term performance expectations
- Must adapt and ensure their organizations adapt to changing expectations and requirements.

As mentioned above, all too often we find that organizations focus on multiple leadership capabilities and measure their leaders on all capabilities. We support that, but we add the following construct: leaders must emphasize specific capabilities/behaviors that are required for the short term—for this particular tack—if they are to ultimately achieve longer-term success. This provides clarity to the organization and to the individual leaders.

Our experience shows that the organization that understands this can execute more effectively.

What we have found in our work with companies large and small is that there are four reasons why people (and therefore, organizations, since organizations are made up of people) don't perform:

- Unaware: They don't know what they are supposed to do
- Unable: They know what they are supposed to do but don't know how to do it
- Constrained: They are aware of what they should do but cannot do it due to process and policy
- Unwilling: They know what they are supposed to do and have the skills and abilities; they just don't want

to do it

This is especially true when we are asking the organization to tack back and forth to achieve its goals. Each question must be answered before (and during) each tack. The worst time to find out that the sailing team does not know how to sail in rough waters is when your next tack brings you there, and the worst thing to do to that team is to ask them to perform in an environment they did not expect and do not understand.

Today's business environment changes rapidly. We need only look at recent history to see this. Financial institutions offer a terrific example. A short time ago, most were focused on driving sales, cross-selling products and services, and aggressively going after new business. The looser regulatory environment encouraged aggressive development of new products, many of which were not understood by the financial wizards themselves. Financial institutions prospered. One of our clients, after a review of their consumer lending process, was flabbergasted that it took upwards of two weeks to review and process a loan application. The directive was to reduce that to two days, and they did. Another client was focused on adding new customers through aggressive financing of property. Their portfolio growth rate almost doubled within 12 months. The board was thrilled!

Then everything changed. Financial institutions, reacting to the financial meltdown of 2008, shifted their focus to process and control, reining in their aggressive growth and sales strategies. They are trying to clean up their balance sheets and loan portfolios. Indeed, the US government is now trying to push financial institutions to start making loans again. This quick shift from aggressive growth and sales to internal focus on quality and process is jolting to an organization and the people in the organization. It is difficult, if not impossible, to get the organization to immediately change its behavior and begin focusing differently, unless leadership has prepared the organization for that. If the organization and its employees understand what is about to change, then change is much easier and quicker. Further, if leadership anticipates the upcoming change, their behavior and focus on key competencies can also change.

Another example is real estate. One of our clients is a major real-estate brokerage. As the housing market tanked, leadership realized that their current approach of aggressively pursuing listings and then sale of those listings would not work. Before the crash, leadership met with the staff and encouraged a "behavior change." No longer would leadership expect listings; what was important was to build and maintain relationships with current clients and future clients (referrals from current clients). With the help of the sales team, this company built an entire new program and approach to help existing clients and prospects understand what was going on in the market, how it impacted their home process, what they could do, and more. Leadership expected this approach to last about 12 months and then wanted to begin "tacking" back to listings. The organization understood that. Leadership clarified what was expected for the next few months and clarified that they would "tack back" to listings soon, and the organization needed to be ready for that.

So the message is clear. In a rapidly changing world, leadership is more challenging. Driving organizational performance requires a continued focus on the tried and true approaches of setting vision and goals, then developing leadership capabilities to drive those goals.

But it now gets a little more complicated. In order to accelerate organizational performance, short-term focus is also required. Long-term success (ultimately the job of leadership) requires execution on short-term deliverables. *Short-term deliverables change during the quest and require different approaches from the organization.*

Our approach to this is a three-step program called Organizational Performance Profiling© System that focuses on identifying and measuring organizational short-term performance needs, leadership capabilities required for success, and individual and team performance.

We assume that leadership is competent and has fully executed a functioning organizational performance/leadership model (What, Why, How, WIFM, or a similar model), and we assume that specific, defined leadership capabilities are in place. We then challenge leadership to define what they need out of the organization within the next three months—how the organization needs to operate—to attain their long-term vision/goals.

Interestingly, we have not had any leader confused by this approach. Quite the contrary, they have been very clear on what they expect to be happening in their organization. What we *have* found is that more often than not, the leadership team itself disagrees over what short-term performance is required. This, of course, means that the leadership needs to overcome this first hurdle before moving on. The leadership team needs to be consistent in its beliefs and approach.

Once consistency is established, we then ask the organization to define how it is actually operating. This almost unerringly leads to a gap in what leadership needs and wants vs. what is actually occurring. Once that is clear, leadership has the ability to set the course straight, and the organization has the ability to define what's getting in the way. This approach greatly accelerates performance against goals.

Concurrent with this process, we have leadership define the leadership competencies most critical to success over the next three months and measure how leadership is performing against those competencies. This allows leadership to develop and focus on key needs.

Finally, we measure individual and team performance to identify accelerators and blockers to short-term-goal attainment.

Simply put, this approach works. It never lets go of the vision and longer-term goals; rather, it focuses short-term activities, which are aligned with those goals, and provides clarity of expectations. It is the quickest path to organizational success, allowing leadership to "tack" while ensuring the organization performs during and after "tacking."

CHAPTER 1

Organizational Performance

Leaders have expectations about how their organizations should work and a clear understanding of the behaviors and disciplines required for success. But is the organization actually operating that way? Too often, the answer is no, and, too often, leaders think the organization is operating as expected when it is not.

Organizations need clear direction. People in an organization must have a solid understanding of where the organization is going and how they (or their team) contribute to that. Further, people need to know what is expected of them when they come to work each day. Absent this, organizations fail.

In our work consulting with senior executives, we have seen that almost every leader—CEO, senior executive, team leader—has a very clear understanding of where she is taking the organization and how she expects her organization or team to operate. Often when we ask the leader to define that, we get very clear answers, such as, "My executive team is focused on execution. They have very specific targets that I expect them to hit, and they are driving performance to attain those targets," or, "My executives are rebuilding our infrastructure, and their focus is to ensure that our systems and processes are sound and efficient. Right now their main goal is to build these processes and controls and ensure they are in place to meet our objectives." The boss knows what she wants and is convinced that her subordinates, and therefore the rest of the organization, are following suit. As a matter of fact, we had a CEO tell us, "If anyone is unclear on what they should be doing and how they should be doing it, send them to me, and I will provide that clarity!"

Leadership, as previously mentioned, is focused on vision and key strategic goals. However, remember that there is another dimension of leadership and organizational performance that, when coupled with the "vision/goals/capabilities" approach, actually *accelerates* organizational performance. When leaders go to the next step—namely, they provide a clear picture of how they expect the organization to perform for the next two to six months—and measure the organization's success against that profile, then organizational performance accelerates.

That's a pretty clear message. It also exemplifies what most CEOs and leaders believe: their direction is clear and they expect their subordinates and the organization to follow that direction. To be sure, we are not implying that all CEOs and leaders are "Pattonesque" in how they give direction and treat subordinates. There are many different leadership styles. However, in our experience, all successful leaders do manifest some common traits, and past research validates that. Jim Collins, in his terrific book, *Good to Great*, articulates leadership characteristics very clearly. He defines "Level 5 leadership"—the top of the ladder—as having the following characteristics:

- Mix of humility and ferocious professional will
- Ability to set up their successors for greater success
- Fanatically driven for results

- Resolved to do whatever it takes to make the company great
- Attribute success factors to other than themselves

Leadership style—whether commanding and forceful, highly relational, or methodically process-oriented—can vary, but successful leaders almost always demonstrate these five traits. Leaders aren't leaders because they want to be liked; they demand respect and move people and organizations to action. They have a commanding knowledge of their company, the market, the competitive landscape, and the organization itself; and they have a vision of where they need to take the company.

James Kouzes and Barry Posner state in *The Leadership Challenge*, "There's nothing more demoralizing than a leader who can't clearly articulate why we're doing what we're doing."

So, this "vision thing" is fundamental to the success of an organization. A leader's vision is where she intends to take the organization. Referencing our model of:

- What
- Why
- How
- WIFM

A leader's vision is the "What." It clarifies where the company is going. Everything the organization does needs to center on attaining that vision.

Once the vision is defined and articulated and understood by everyone, good leaders attach broad, strategic goals to the vision, creating a framework of what they believe the organization needs to do—the mileposts along the way, some steps that must be taken and measured. Jim Collins, in *Good to Great*, calls these "BOHAGs"—Big Old Hairy Audacious Goals. Many of our clients refer to them as strategic goals, the high-level goals around which all subsequent goals and plans are built. The vision and strategic goals are fundamental in setting the foundation for successful organizations. Everyone in the organization needs to understand these and ensure that what they are doing every day links directly to the attainment of these strategic goals. If not, their activities need to be questioned.

This is a rather straightforward process: leadership establishes a clear vision and strategic goals. It's a process that consultants love because we can challenge the goals developed downstream and help "tighten" them for better alignment, thereby improving organizational productivity. We often find that communication of the vision and/or strategic goals is misunderstood or, even worse, not communicated at all! This makes for interesting work for us because we can then get involved with helping develop communication programs as well as work with clients to help ensure that reward systems are aligned.

The importance of communicating the vision and goals is critical. Further, the importance of clearly defining short-term results and behavioral expectations is critical to obtaining the long-term vision. People simply need to know "what" is expected of them *today* in order to achieve the overall vision. It is critical that leadership ensures that the actions of the organization are indeed focused on the vision and goals. Further, it is important that the actions of the organization are relatively consistent, behaviorally, to the leader's expectations. For example, if leadership is expecting the organization to aggressively pursue sales results, then the sales team needs to be out selling, not completing forms and doing other administrative or process work.

We typically encounter two fundamental disconnects that result in lower-than-expected results:

- The leader and her executive team disagree with how the organization should be operating.

This is a huge problem because typically the executive team is, in fact, pulling toward the same goal—the "What." The problem is that each member has a different idea of how to get there, resulting in mixed messaging to the organization and poor organizational performance.

- The organization is operating differently than leadership expects.

This can result from a number of things. Obviously, if leadership is providing mixed messages, then the organization will seek its own way. Another issue could be that organizational blockers exist—policy and procedure, technology limitations, etc. Leadership needs to be aware of these and address them if organizational performance is to improve. A typical example of an organizational blocker could be the focus on cost containment vs. revenue generation. Operations, the backbone of making an organization work, needs to operate as efficiently as possible; but this sometimes becomes the key driving force, sacrificing the focus on revenue generation. Leadership needs to ensure that the organization understands the primary focus and is operating to that end.

We encounter both of these issues in almost every

organization. While everyone has the right intent and is totally committed to the vision and strategic goals—and have developed "downstream" goals consistent with the strategic goals—the reality is that the organization will not perform at peak level because leadership has not focused on the "How." Simply stated:

- In addition to defining the vision and strategic goals—the "What"—leadership must articulate how the organization needs to pursue those goals: the "How."

This is where leadership can take the organization to the next level of performance. By clearly defining how the organization should operate, people know and understand what they need to do and how they need to do it.

Let's get into this a little deeper.

We'll provide a simple model for organizational performance.

Organizational performance involves three distinct but interrelated disciplines, all of which are required for success. The three disciplines are:

Competitive, Controlling, and Connective

Competitive is defined as focusing on results and delivering expected outcomes—a focused, targeted, driven, risk-taking, goal-oriented, and persevering organization. Organizations stressing these disciplines have clearly established business objectives, a strong sales mentality, an active and aggressive performance-management system, and a pay-for-performance standard. A *competitive culture* is usually opportunistic, energetic, and intense. There are consequences for success and failure and clarity of what has to be done and by when.

The positive attributes of a competitive culture include actions that promote execution, delivery, timeliness, action-oriented perspective, innovation, and high leader-driven expectations. Competitive cultures prefer change that is transformational. They are highly adaptive in fast-changing environments, externally focused, and acquisitive in nature. Things are happening fast. Failure is ok, but you have to get up and keep going. Success is measured by action and speed.

Controlling can be defined as focusing on process, structure, and order. The focus is analytical, practical, methodical—a metric-based organization. Teams bolstering this discipline are driving process improvement, metrics and analytics, reporting, and clarity of process. Documenting outcomes and analyzing results of actions are paramount to the culture.

Positive aspects include a bias toward being more factual, more structured, more numerically report-driven, more focused on tracking, more committed to a scientific approach, more technology-dependent, more uniform in action, more able to use monitoring, and more routine oriented, practical, and methodical. Controlling cultures prefer growth that is slow and transitional in nature. Growth is episodic, planned, organized, measured…in short, ordered. These organizations can be perceived as slow moving and not adapting to change, especially by competitive-oriented leaders. These organizations focus on "measure twice, cut once."

Connective can be defined as focusing on the interactive nature of work and includes behaviors such as involvement, relationship, and collective effort. These organizations promote an approach that is systemic and holistically oriented, concerned with how things "fit" or do not "fit" together. Additional descriptors associated with *connective* include: experience (experiential), community, intuition, and cooperation. When the connective discipline is emphasized, the organization focuses on a more inclusive perspective: how people are working together, how people and processes are functioning, and how well the parts are working within the whole. Connective companies review the morale of the organization, the needs of all constituencies, the level and quality of communication within the established networks, etc.

Connective cultures prefer organizational growth that is developmental in nature—a change that is emergent and incremental—with an aim to enhance or improve existing practices. Connective growth is conservative at its foundation. These types of organizations can be perceived as complex because everything needs to be considered prior to action.

In summary, organizational performance requires a focus on three interrelated disciplines:

- Competitive focus
  - Results
  - Delivering expected outcomes
  - Opportunistic, energetic and intense, focused, targeted, driven, risk-taking, and goal-oriented activities
- Controlling focus
  - Process
  - Structure and order
  - Logical, analytical, and metric-focused activities
- Connective focus
  - Involvement

3C© Performance Modeling

- Relationship
- Working together, broad outlook and perspective, inclusive activities

There is no right or optimum order for these three disciplines. Rather, the business environment, competitive pressures, stage of organizational growth, etc. drive one or another to the forefront. Additionally, successful organizations can quickly switch emphasis—or "tack"—when necessary to ensure short-term focus is on the critical need. This promotes better operation in rapidly changing environments. While all three disciplines are vital, one has priority in the order. However, a balance is necessary.

Let's look at a few examples.

An organization that is focused on building infrastructure and internal controls for the next two months in order to position itself for a major sales effort might look something like this:

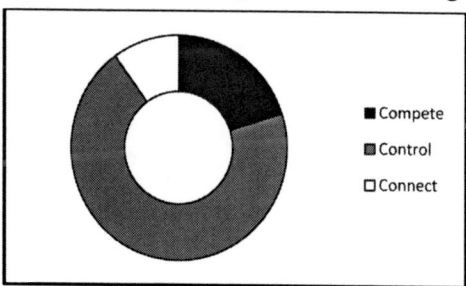

[Pie chart showing: ■ Compete, ■ Control, □ Connect]

As you can see, the primary focus is on *control* disciplines; however, the focus on results and *connect* have not been abandoned. Indeed, there is still focus on connect and competitive to ensure that, while internal controls and processes are being formalized, internal teams are also working on building relationships to encourage collaboration as well as execution.

Once the controls and processes are established, leadership will want to pivot the organization to focus on execution and results—namely, a more competitive focus—while simultaneously starting to leverage those internal relationships. This profile could look like this:

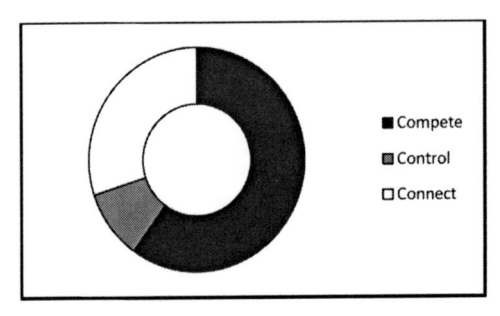

[Donut chart showing three segments labeled: ■ Compete, ■ Control, □ Connect]

As you can see, the primary focus is execution and results now that the processes are in place, with a continued secondary emphasis on leveraging internal departments.

This is an example of how leadership can shift the focus of an organization on a short-term basis to ensure that long-term vision and goals are accomplished. In this case, attempting to move immediately to execution without the internal controls, processes, and working relationships built would not result in required performance. Leadership recognized what needed to be done, focused the organization on short-term outcomes, provided a simple tool/language (the Performance Profile system), and ultimately moved the organization more quickly.

All three disciplines are needed for success, but most organizations focus on one or two, and often the focus is inconsistent with the disciplines required by the leader.

Out of Balance

Typically, an organization emphasizes one discipline over the others, dependent on current pressures. That does not exclude focus on the other two disciplines, however. For example, it could be argued that during the financial crisis of 2008, many financial institutions were focusing on the *control* discipline more than *competitive* or *connective*; they were focused on ensuring that their credit-review policies and procedures were strong, that systems were in place to flag problems, and that financial process was strong. But they still sold and still continued to build relationships. It's just that the *control* discipline had moved to the forefront. Soon, these institutions would swing back to more competitive behavior, with a higher focus on sales and growth.

Organizations can, however, overreact; they can move a discipline to the forefront and completely ignore one of the other disciplines. We call this being "out of balance." When the organization focuses on a discipline to the exclusion of one or both of the other disciplines, that organization is out of balance, and performance suffers mightily.

A competitive organization that is out of balance is one that creates change for change's sake. Have you ever seen an organization where goals and objectives change daily? People don't know what to do, so they wait. The constant movement (forward, backward, to a new goal/objective) results in few accomplishments. The company's efforts are scattered. This rushed and chaotic environment—while energizing to some—can be too uncontrolled for others. Additional downside attributes of a competitive-accentuated culture include unrealistic objectives, capacity to ignore planning and steps, stubbornness, and a sense of being obsessive, elitist, and overly demanding. An out-of-balance organization may look like this:

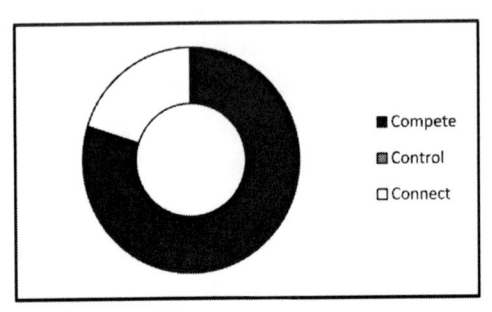

- Compete
- Control
- Connect

As you can see from this profile, the organization is almost completely focused on the competitive behaviors, with no attention to control and little focus on connect. This is an organization that will push only for results, despite what those results may bring. Ultimately, this profile leads to performance failure because goals and execution become a moving target for everyone.

A controlling organization that is out of balance is one that is obsessive with documentation, data, process, and analysis. The organization is prone to slow movement or inaction due to the need for constant measures. A company highlighting this discipline risks being too myopic, too rigid, and too overly controlling in its behavior. Consequences include a myopic perspective, a sense of being shackled by process or procedure, and becoming robotic, monotonous, overly controlling, unimaginative, and rigid.

3C© Performance Modeling

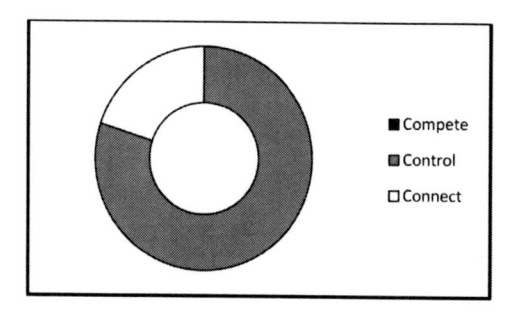

> ■ Compete
> ▨ Control
> ☐ Connect

    As you can see from this profile, the emphasis is on the *control* discipline, resulting in an organization that will continue to analyze and create plans but will never execute against those plans.

    Finally, a connective organization that is out of balance is one that is prone to making things too unstructured. Decisions tend to be made out of a sense of sentimentality or based on subjective rather than objective information and data. Often hampered by few—if any—standards, the company's performance suffers. There are few repercussions for objectives not being met. Organizations that focus exclusively on *connect* run the risk of experiencing a culture that is overly complicated, tends to neglect specifics, is too subjective, can be prone to dependency formation, prone to a loss of individuality, is apt to lose discreet parts/pieces, and is faltering in a clear ability to discriminate true priorities.

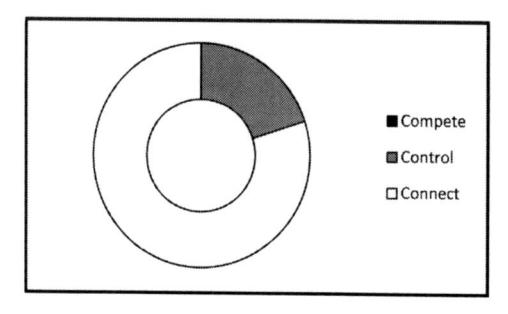

> ■ Compete
> ▨ Control
> ☐ Connect

13

This profile will lead to a highly congenial, caring organization that gets nothing done.

Again, all three disciplines are important for success.

As you can see, an out-of-balance situation is dangerous; the company falters, and it must be put back on track quickly. The good news is that by using performance-profiling methodology, the organization can quickly learn that it is out of balance and begin the change to get properly focused. The Performance Profile provides a picture of the desired stated leadership needs and a language to help the organization quickly transition to that state.

Let's look at an example of how the G2's Organizational Performance Profile accelerates organizational performance.

The G2 Organizational Performance Profiling tool has been used in many companies with tremendous success. It provides a quick (30 minute) assessment of the organization and results in three key outcomes:

1. A picture of how the leader expects the organization to operate
2. A picture of how the leadership *team* expects the organization to operate (this ensures harmony among the leadership team)
3. A picture of how the organization is actually operating

In our experience we rarely find consistency. Further, this inconsistency results in performance degradation—the organization is simply not performing at its peak because everyone is not rowing in the same direction. The leader called for the boat to "tack," but no one was ready...and some on the leadership team thought the boat should *not* "tack!"

The process for the organizational profile is straightforward:

3C© Performance Modeling

1. The leader (CEO, executive, or team leader) completes the Performance Profile questionnaire outlining how the organization *should* operate
2. The leadership team completes the same questionnaire, defining how the organization *should* operate
3. The organization completes the questionnaire defining how the organization *is* operating

This simple process results in a graphic representation of how each group—the leader, the leadership team, and the organization—views the organization relative to the focus required on competitive, controlling, and connective disciplines.

Results can look like this:

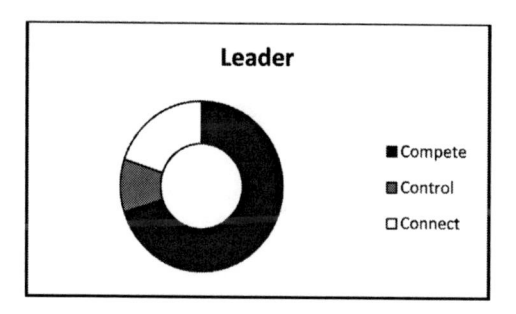

Leader

- Compete
- Control
- Connect

Profile of leader compared to leadership team:

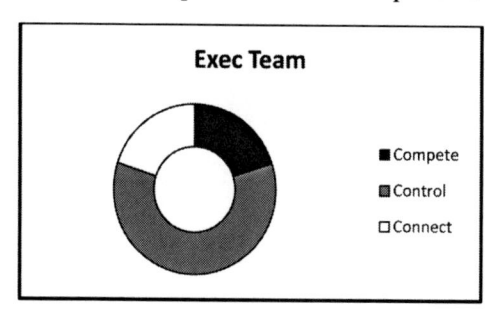

Exec Team

- Compete
- Control
- Connect

15

As you can see, the leader is calling for a higher focus on competitive—moving to execution and delivery—while her leadership team is more focused on the control disciplines.

The first step is to align everyone to ensure a common profile from leadership. Obviously, if the senior team is not in agreement about how it expects the organization to operate, then mixed messages will be sent to the organization resulting in suboptimal performance.

Once leadership agrees on the common profile—how the organization *should* operate—then we compare that to the profile of how the organization is actually operating.

Here is the comparison of the leadership profile to the organization's actual profile:

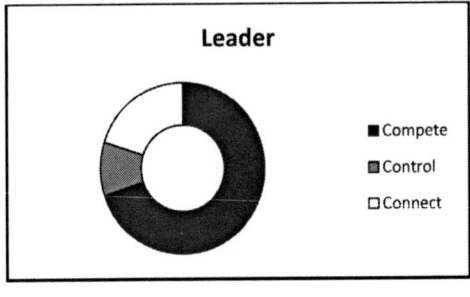

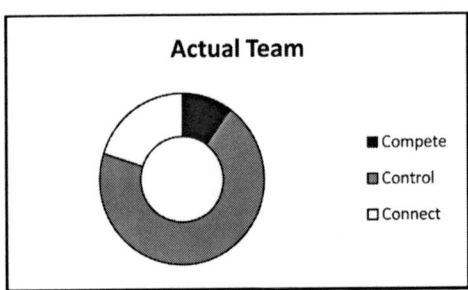

Leader
- Compete
- Control
- Connect

Actual Team
- Compete
- Control
- Connect

You can readily see a disconnect. The organization remains focused on control disciplines rather then moving to execution.

This allows the leader to communicate the requirement to move to a new focus and allows the organization to identify what's getting in the way and ultimately move to the new profile.

So, if we summarize the results of the process, we can state the following:

- Competitive discipline scores low
  - **– Impact**
    - Uncomfortable taking risk
    - Low focus on winning and achieving goals
    - Unable to move quickly to meet business needs
    - Limited innovation
    - Low accountability
    - Slow to act/change

- Control discipline scores high
  - **– Impact**
    - Role clarity is critical before action is taken
    - Goal alignment necessary before action
    - Process critical before action
    - Slow decisions/movement
    - Status quo–oriented

- Connection discipline is moderately high
  - **– Impact**
    - Team is comfortable collaborating
    - Focus on customer is recognized

We can conclude that:
Leadership and senior management are not aligned. This can result in many consequences, including:
- Confused messaging and expectations between leadership and management
- Incorrect leadership behaviors
- Below-par results

Leadership, management, and staff are not aligned relative to the behaviors and methodologies defined for success. The impact is:
- Confusion in communication of performance expectations, skill assessment, and individual performance
- Negative impact on business performance.

Leadership and the staff are not aligned, *not only* around which discipline is most critical at this junction but also the order of priority in general. The consequences of this can include:
- Time/energy spent in wrong behaviors, negatively impacting performance
- Skills-development needs improperly focused
- Lack of focus on key skill-performance needs

In a quick, 30-minute questionnaire, the CEO was able to see that her organization had some problems that had to be addressed.

The Performance Profile provided four significant outcomes:

1. A clear picture of how the organization "should be" operating as defined by the CEO

3C© Performance Modeling

2. The revelation of a disconnect between the CEO and her executive team on how the organization "should be operating"
3. A picture of how the organization is actually operating
4. A simple language for the organization to use to quickly move to the desired state

Of course, the first step was to get the CEO and her team aligned. The profile output allowed for significant discussion about the disconnect among the leadership team and allowed them to ultimately determine the profile they could all support. This built a united team using a common "picture" of how the organization was expected to operate. This is a strong message to an organization and leaves no room for misinterpretation.

The second step was to present the desired profile to each subgroup/team in the organization and compare that to their specific results. This resulted in two key outcomes:

1. Leadership presented the "What" and the "Why"—they presented the model they wanted and why that model was important
2. The team was expected to generate the "How"—what they needed to do to move to the new model.

The bottom line is this: the organization was now properly focused on precisely what leadership needed them to do.

Now let's repeat something here: we are talking about short-term, what leadership needs the organization to do within the next three to six months. When leadership focuses the organization on what is to be accomplished and how it is to be accomplished within the next two to six months, the organization is focused on delivering those results, thereby accelerating delivery of longer-term results.

The Performance Profile allows leadership to continually redefine or reemphasize how the organization needs to be performing. It provides a clear, simple picture of leadership expectations and allows the organization to focus on meeting those expectations.

The outcomes are straightforward:

1. An executive team profile aligned with the direction and expectations of its leader
2. A team focused on operating efficiently and effectively given the key goals it needs to accomplish

Further, leadership can easily change focus rapidly. Let's use our financial-services example: After the financial meltdown, banks focused on credit process and quality, loan-portfolios systems, and operational integrity. But soon they needed to change their focus to a more balanced approach, raising the competitive-disciplines line. The language of the Performance Profile allows for a quicker transition.

Let's take another example. In this instance, our client was an 18-month-old marketing and exhibit house that was growing at a dramatic pace, due in large part to its hard-driving and entrepreneurial leadership team. This group, all industry veterans, joined forces to introduce an innovative concept in the business, combining the creative aspects of exhibit design with integrated marketing and manufacturing capabilities. This "just in time" capability enabled faster turnaround for clients and provided them with a market advantage. To further differentiate themselves, they provided "rental" services, whereby they had modular exhibit sets that could be combined in differing combinations that they would customize with graphics and

3C© Performance Modeling

color schemes to meet clients' needs.

When we first met with the CEO, he was concerned that the firm had hit a plateau and wanted to move the organization to the next level of performance. He believed one problem was inefficiency, which hurt their productivity. When we asked him about the level of understanding employees had regarding the company's vision and strategy, he was quite confident that everyone was clear. As a matter of fact, his comment was, "Communication is one of our greatest strengths." That claim was tested by the Performance Profile and, in fact, the perception from the employees' perspective was quite different.

Leadership had come to recognize that the high risk–tolerant behaviors that enabled them to create, build, and launch their company needed to be replaced with a more systematic approach to their work. Indeed, the leadership team knew almost instinctively that they were inefficient because they lacked a more standardized, disciplined, and project-based methodology in virtually all aspects of their work. This mentality led to employees pursuing multiple avenues for achieving the same result. Inefficiency was rampant because the company was constantly recreating processes and procedures because they had no structure.

Leadership was looking for more *control*.

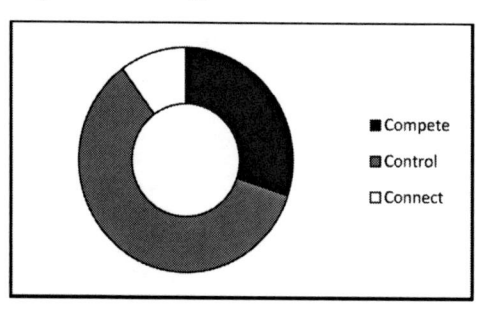

Although the leadership team was relatively aligned behind their sense of how the company should operate, the employees saw a very different picture.

From the employees' perspective, the company was primarily focused on sales, growth, and closed contracts.

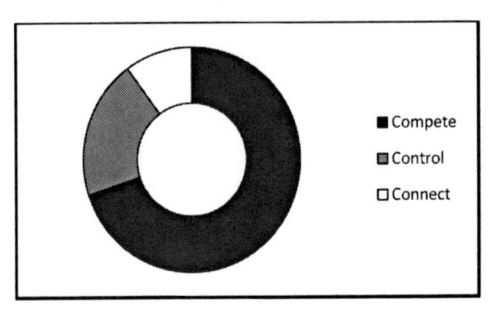

[Donut chart showing Compete, Control, Connect]

Their results were skewed toward the *compete* aspects of the Performance Profile and indicated that the *control* and *connect* attributes were underemphasized. Summarizing the results of this assessment, we can state the following:

- Leadership and staff were not aligned relative to the behaviors and methodologies defined for success.
  - **Consequences**
    - Confusion in communication of performance expectations, skill assessment, individual performance
    - Negative impact on business performance
- Leadership and the staff were not aligned, *not only* around which discipline is most critical at this junction but also the order of priority in general.

3C© Performance Modeling

– Consequences

- ☐ Time/energy spent in wrong behaviors, negatively impacting performance
- ☐ Skills-development needs improperly focused
- ☐ Lack of focus on key skill-performance needs

One final example. In this engagement we were working with an established web-based business that provided products and services that enabled customers to do in-depth research. Once again, the leadership team felt confident that they were in "lock-step" on the key priorities for the business. When we deployed the Performance Profile, we dove into three layers of the management structure: the head of operations (leader), the head of the research division (senior management), and a team leader in the Client Services Division (manager). In addition, we had an intact call-center team complete the Performance Profile in order to compare the leadership team's desired state to the actual state as perceived by the employees.

The results of using the 30-minute Organizational Performance Profiling tool showed the following:

A high disconnect existed between the leader and his management team, where the leader was calling for strong *connect* profile to drive collaboration, customer focus, and a secondary focus on *compete*—driving performance to meet objectives. The executive team focused differently, calling for greater emphasis on *control*.

The impact of this is obvious. A confusing message is delivered to the organization; namely, the leader stating one thing but his managers acting on something different. People in the organization will be confused, and performance will suffer.

In summary, the Performance Profile's strength is its simplistic ability to compare and contrast the messages being sent and received within an organization. The effectiveness of those messages is directly related to the actions employees take on a daily basis—what they are focused on, what they are prioritizing, and what they are delivering. When everyone within a company is pulling in the same direction—"tacking" at the same time—then the boat turns quickly, captures the wind, and moves faster on course. However, most organizations, in our experience, don't set their sails as effectively as they could. G2's Performance Profile provides a visual that enables leaders to correct course and rally their employees toward the new direction.

CHAPTER 2

Defined Leadership

We stated that it is imperative that leaders set a vision, establish strategic goals, and align "downstream" goals and activities to ensure that the organization's actions are moving the company toward attaining the vision and goals. Further, we have shown the importance of short-term focus; namely, ensuring the organization is actually doing what leadership expects and, of course, that the leadership team is demonstrating clear and consistent alignment regarding its expectations.

Using the Organizational Profiling System outlined in Chapter 1, leadership has the ability to continually adjust and measure the behavior and focus of the organization. Additionally, the organization has clarity of what is expected and can work to accomplish that or to identify any blockers that may exist so leadership can remove those blockers. Our experience is that when leadership provides a clear picture of what it expects from the organization in the next three to six months and the organization understands that and has the opportunity to tell leadership what's getting in the way, then the organization moves forward at an accelerated rate—translation: the organization performs better.

This all depends on leadership, however. So let's take a few minutes and talk about leadership. Just what *is* leadership?

John Kotter explains it this way in *Leading Change*: "Managers do things right, leaders do the right things."

Kouzes and Posner take it a step further in *The Leadership*

Challenge by actually defining what the "right things" are:
- Model the way
- Inspire a shared vision
- Challenge the process
- Enable others to act
- Encourage the heart

These are very dramatic statements of what is expected of leaders! They provide a very clear understanding that leadership behavior is indeed critical to the success of the organization. We know that change is not possible without the "buy in" from people in the organization; they really have to understand and believe in the new vision and goals, and they need to understand and believe that the short-term goals that leadership expects are indeed connected and appropriate.

The way to help ensure this is through modeling—that is, leaders "model" the appropriate behavior. This is absolutely critical.

Before the "desired profile" can be presented to an organization, the entire leadership team must be in full agreement, and the team must model the behaviors associated with that profile.

Stated simply, leadership teams need to:
- Ensure clarity of tasks and responsibilities of the leadership team
- Unite around a common message
- Display behaviors and actions directly tied to organizational performance expectations

This will lead to a leadership team that:
- Speaks with one voice
- Models how the organization needs to behave and perform
- Energizes and transforms the organization

Note the second bullet above—a team that models how the organization needs to behave and perform. This is a fundamental requirement for top organizational performance. As we highlighted in our examples, when leadership does not model the behavior it expects, the organization is given permission to behave differently, and it will.

Further, it is our experience that leadership can and should change its behavior given the short-term behavior it requires from the organization. For example, if it is necessary to fix process and policy before initiating an aggressive sales campaign, then leadership must display those behaviors and actions linked to improving/fixing process. Once the process is fixed, then leadership behavior can move to the execution model.

Most of the top-performing companies we have worked with have identified leadership capabilities and behaviors required for success. Many have processes in place to evaluate their leaders on these capabilities, and they focus on developing these capabilities in leaders. Some have 15 or 20 capabilities and related behaviors; others have as few as three or four. This approach works—and works well.

In our experience we have found that companies with defined leadership capabilities and related behaviors have stronger leadership teams.

We have also found that leadership rarely uses all

capabilities at any given time; rather, the focus is on one or two capabilities to achieve short-term results. In a world of constant, fast change, today's leadership capabilities can become tomorrow's vulnerabilities. Sometimes leaders can focus on the wrong capabilities, given what the organization's performance requirements demand.

For example, using our story of an organization that needs to tighten its process and policy before implementing an aggressive sales campaign, leadership would need to focus on behaviors and capabilities that promote process improvement, analytics, reporting, etc. If a particular leader were focused instead on driving the organization for results (perhaps because it was a preferred style for that leader), then the organization would be receiving a mixed message about how it is expected to behave, resulting in suboptimum performance. Conversely, if the organization had already fixed the process and infrastructure and was ready to execute, and leadership behavior was modeling process control, methodology, reporting and analytics…well, you can see the impact. Leadership must model the behavior it needs from the organization.

This calls for a new twist on leadership performance and behavior—namely, that leaders must be capable of "flexible" behavior. Leaders must be able to model different leadership styles and behaviors at varying times, dependent on what they require from the organization. Given the rapid pace of change in today's markets and the approach we have been stating regarding moving the organization along in short-term increments, it would be crazy to change leaders every three months. It is clear that to be effective, leaders must have the ability to demonstrate different styles/behaviors if they are to be successful at building high-performing organizations.

So just what are the key capabilities and behaviors that leaders must use? As we stated previously, many organizations have already developed leadership capabilities and related behaviors, and we are not promoting the abandonment of these. Rather, our experience shows that when leadership teams focus on those attributes and behaviors that support the current expectations of the organization—in other words, when leadership *models* the actions and behaviors it expects of the organization—then organizational performance improves. This is a fundamental concept of organizational performance: leadership must model the behavior it expects from the organization.

The key is to apply this modeling to the *immediate* need.

Using our organizational profiling model—competitive behaviors, controlling behaviors, and connective behaviors—it follows that leaders must align their actions with the actions they expect/need from the organization. So if leadership has determined that the organization needs to be focused on "controlling" disciplines for the next two to three months, it is imperative for leadership to model that behavior by focusing on those capabilities that are more closely aligned with "controlling" disciplines. Or if leadership has determined that it needs to quickly move the organization to more "competitive" disciplines with a high focus on results and execution, then leadership needs to model those attributes and behaviors more closely aligned with execution and delivery.

We call this "Defined Leadership." We are actually defining the type of modeling required from leadership to effectively move the organization to the desired behaviors.

Let's look at an example. We recently completed work with an organization that was looking to improve the level of sales and service they were providing to their top-tier clients. In developing the program the company could implement to engage employees, we encouraged the leader to articulate his vision for employees. Using the Performance Profile, leadership was able to provide a simple, quick picture of how the organization needed to operate; namely, results and execution—competitive disciplines. The "actual" profile completed by the organization showed that the organization was highly focused on the control disciplines, completely understandable since leadership had spent the previous four months developing new processes and controls to allow for the upcoming sales focus. Once the organization understood the new requirement, they met in teams to identify potential and real blockers to transitioning to the new competitive approach. In one meeting, employees provided a number of examples of how the policy was actually hampering the company's ability to retain customers, remain competitive, and cross-sell other services. The leader asked if others were having the same experience, and after three more employees shared similar experiences, the leader raised his hand and announced, "Effective immediately, the policy will no longer be a part of the decision process and, with the right forms of verification, employees can approve sales within a defined range on the spot." This was modeling competitive leadership behaviors. The announcement was met with disbelief, followed by euphoria. After the excitement died down, we took a moment to note how the leader had just done what he was looking for from others: taking calculated risks. Not only did the leadership demonstrate the behaviors required, but by doing this, he empowered others to do it, thereby moving the organization to the new model more quickly.

As you can see, when the correct behavior is modeled, the organization sees and follows. There is clarity. Remember: nothing undermines organizational effort and performance more than leadership behavior that is different from or inconsistent with stated expectations. Let's take a quick review of the 3C Organizational Performance Profile.

The 3C Organizational Performance Profile requires a focus on three interrelated disciplines:

– **Competitive focus**
  - Results
  - Delivering expected outcomes
  - Opportunistic, energetic and intense, focused, targeted, driven, risk-taking, and goal-oriented activities

– **Controlling focus**
  - Process
  - Structure and order
  - Logical, analytical, and metric-focused activities

– **Connective focus**
  - Involvement
  - Relationship
  - Working together, broad outlook and perspective, inclusive activities

There is no right or optimum order for these three disciplines. Rather, the business environment, competitive pressures, stages of organizational growth, etc. drive one or another to the forefront and establish the precedence given to those behaviors that are necessary for growth, stability, or change. While all three disciplines are vital, one has priority in the order. However, a balance is necessary.

All three disciplines are needed for success, but most organizations focus on one or two, and often the focus is inconsistent with the disciplines required by the leader.

Defined Leadership links leadership capabilities and behaviors to each C, allowing leaders to see the specific capabilities and behaviors that properly model each performance discipline.

Organizations that already have capabilities will find no problem linking their leadership attributes to these. As a matter of fact, we have worked with many organizations where we have substituted their proprietary capabilities, thereby maintaining direct connection to balanced scorecards and other performance programs already in place. Other organizations have used the capabilities we provided and have implemented them, evaluating their leaders around the dimensions we provided.

However you decide to proceed, the key is linking leadership capabilities and behaviors with the organizational performance expectations.

Let's look at the three different leadership-capability summaries. We'll start by simply listing typical attributes for each type of leader.

Competitive Leader

Curious, aggressive, risk taker, self-confident, opportunistic, energetic, strategic, innovative, persuasive, powerful, intuitive, warrior, credible, dominant, impatient, activist,

3C© Performance Modeling

intentional, independent, willful, relentless, determined, forceful, dynamic, commanding.

Controlling Leader

Rational, consistent, competent, intentional, steadfast, tactical, self-disciplined, reliable, persistent, incremental, measured, logical, objective, negotiator, realistic, profit-driven, deal maker, risk manager, mathematic, methodical, planner, solid, tough, steadfast.

Connective Leader

Systemic, cautious, traditionalist, process-oriented, friendly, networker, creative, innovative, empathic, discerning, contextual, flexible, ideational, facilitative, compromiser, political, nuanced, diplomatic, assertive listener, advocate, communicator, group builder, relationship tracker, insightful, reframes ideas.

These represent the various attributes or descriptors for leadership behaviors relative to the three profiles. Remember, true leaders must be capable of operating with all three styles, emphasizing one more than the other two (but not losing the other two completely and becoming out of balance) where appropriate. Leaders must be able to smoothly transition from one style to another to effectively model the behaviors they expect of the organization. Not only do they need to do this at an organizational level but also at an individual level. Dealing with different types of people requires style change. More on that later.

We have no evidence that one style is better than any other. There are many who mistakenly believe that leaders must be forceful and focused on driving an organization to solid results—a competitive-style orientation. This is not the case. Many successful leaders exhibit differing styles, and almost all of them can emphasize different styles when needed.

Let's look at a couple of examples.

General Eisenhower is perhaps a good personification of a control-oriented leader. He focused on planning, preparation, and analysis. That was his comfort zone and his preferred approach. However, on June 6, 1944, when it was time to go, he went, switching to the competitive profile and thus ensuring his army charged ahead.

Abraham Lincoln could be a good personification of the connective leader, one who surrounded himself with people who supported him and people who did not. He sought all input. But again, when he was ready to go, he pushed to the competitive side. Toward the end of the war he was moving to connective—joining the country in reconstruction and togetherness.

These are but two examples of leaders who may be more comfortable in one discipline (as we all are) but who could easily move from one discipline to another when necessary to move the organization forward.

We have demonstrated that leaders have expectations about how their organizations should work. They have clear understanding of the behaviors and disciplines required for success. We have also demonstrated that, too often, leaders think the organization is operating as expected when it is not.

Organizations need clear direction. People in an organization must have a solid understanding of where the organization is going and how they (or their team) contribute to that. People must know what is expected of them today.

Absent this, organizations fail.

We have reasoned that organizational performance involves three distinct but interrelated disciplines, all required for success—competitive, controlling, and connective.

Further, we contend that organizations continually shift the focus on these disciplines—much like a sailboat tacking back and forth—to attain their vision and strategic goals. We have stated that it is leadership's job to ensure the organization is properly focused and is acting appropriately over the short term to deliver long-term results.

Finally, we have stated the obvious—namely, that leadership must model the behaviors they expect from their people if they are to get maximum performance from the organization.

Aligning leadership capabilities and behaviors with the required behaviors of the organization is the fundamental key to success.

We can therefore come up with a "Leadership Competency Model"—defining the leadership behaviors required for the various performance disciplines.

Leadership Competency Model

G2 Partners' Organizational Performance Profile and Leadership Competency Model allows leaders to clearly define how they expect their organization to operate and compare those expectations to what is actually happening and also to focus their energies on leadership skills to drive success.

The 3C Leadership Model is built around three macro disciplines, all of which are required for success but require different levels of intensity based on situational needs.

1. A focused, targeted, driven, risk-taking, goal-oriented,

and persevering organization. Organizations stressing these disciplines, defined as competitive, have clearly established business objectives, a strong sales mentality, an active performance-management effort, and a pay-for-performance standard.

2. An analytical, practical, methodical, and metric-based organization. Teams bolstering this discipline of controlling are driving process improvement, metrics and analytics, reporting, and clarity of process.

3. A focus on the interactive nature of work, including behaviors such as involvement, relationship, and collective effort. These organizations promote a connective approach, systemic and holistically oriented—concerned with how things "fit" or do not "fit" together.

All three disciplines are needed for success, but most organizations focus on one or two, and often the focus is not consistent with the disciplines required by the leader. It is critical for the leader to define the desired focus and to employ the appropriate leadership competencies and behaviors to drive performance toward that discipline.

Leaders must be competent in all three disciplines and must be able to emphasize the leadership competencies of each discipline at various levels of focus. Additionally, leaders must never—repeat, never—abandon any discipline completely. Rather, it is a matter of focus. They must be able to focus on a particular discipline more strongly and be able to shift to another very quickly.

The competencies and role examples of each discipline follow:

Competitive Leader

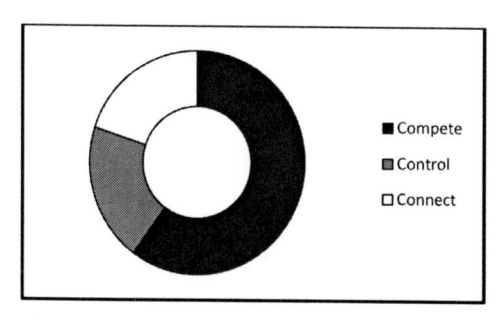

[Pie chart showing: Compete, Control, Connect]

Organizational Performance Expectations

A focused, targeted, driven, risk-taking, goal-oriented, and persevering organization focused on results and delivery.

Core Competencies of a Competitive-Oriented Leader

1. Sets clear, bold goals
2. Drives change; seeks opportunities
3. Visionary
4. Drives performance and execution
5. Maintains motivating pressure on businesses and people
6. Delivers results
7. High risk tolerance

Key Roles

Market Opportunist: Uncovers business opportunities through a continuing attraction to the new and different, a willingness to take risks.

Action-Oriented Thought Leader: Capacity to see things in a new way.

Intuitive Marketer: Comprehends the overall market situation without the necessity of detailed information or data.

Courageous Change Agent: Commits an organization to new and significant actions despite uncertainty and resistance.

Product Champion: Manifests courage to bring new products/ services to the market before a clear need is recognized.

Improviser: Can shift direction strategically and decisively to meet new conditions in the market.

Motivator: Secures personal loyalty and involvement of others.

Drives Others: Stimulates enthusiastic involvement of others in order to achieve the organizational mission.

Control Leader

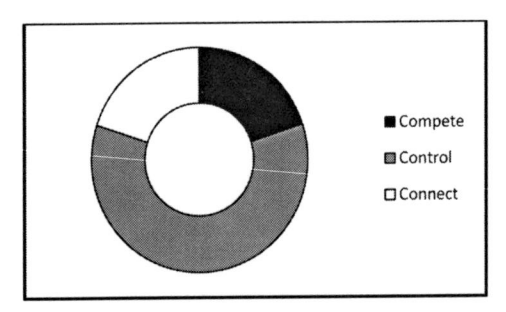

Organizational Performance Expectations

Focus on process improvement, metrics and analytics, reporting, and clarity of process, metric-based, analytical, cautious.

3C© Performance Modeling

Core Competencies of a Controlling-Oriented Leader
1. Analytical
2. Pragmatic; sets realistic goals
3. Process-focused
4. Methodical
5. Ability to develop and manage plans
6. Quality-focused
7. Persistent

Key Roles

Responsible Delegator: Gives needed authority to employees in a clear, precise manner while maintaining overall control.

Goal Overseer: Someone who believes in the importance of goals and uses them to manage the organization.

Organization-Stability Manager: A leader who maintains a healthy balance between processes bringing change and those bringing stability in an organization.

Implementer: Leads an organization toward its specific goals by designing workflow, focusing resources, evaluating progress, and accepting overall responsibility for the results of others' efforts.

Efficiency Expert: Always seeking to improve efficiency.

Performance Evaluator: Recognizes performance gaps and takes steps to correct.

Connective Leader

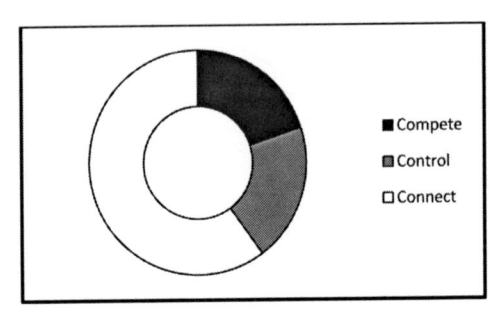

[Donut chart showing: Compete, Control, Connect]

Organizational Performance Expectations

A focus on the interactive nature of work, high involvement, relationship, and a collective effort. A systemic and holistic orientation; concerned with how things "fit" or do not "fit" together.

Core Competencies of a Connective-Oriented Leader

1. Imaginative—can see many opportunities and relationships
2. Highly diplomatic
3. Generates ideas for others
4. Relationship builder
5. Champions harmony and consistency toward goals
6. Collaborative
7. Values diversity and different perspectives

Key Roles

Organizational Mentor: Encourages others to recognize, develop, and use their personal resources.

Learning Enthusiast: Radiates desire for personal growth and challenge.

Conceptual Persuader: Uses ideas and concepts to persuade others to a point of view or a decision.

Relationship Reader: Accurately assesses relationships in an organization and uses the information wisely in planning courses of action.

Harmonic-Solution Provider: Develops solutions that respect and care for all the elements of the organizational system.

System Monitor: Watches the balance and alignment of the organization as a system.

Counselor: Accessible to discuss problems and provide guidance.

Persuader: Influences influential people in an organization through intuitive awareness and persistence.

G2 Partners' Defined Leadership program focuses on identifying the key leadership capabilities and behaviors required for immediate *and* long-term success. It is a process to link leadership performance to required business results and leaves the organization with the capability to grow and modify leadership capabilities as market forces demand change.

Defined Leadership is a customized service that enables executives to clearly define the specific behaviors required to lead their organization forward. G2 Partners provides a structured process that gives clients the tools necessary for defining their unique leadership attributes, a method for assessing current capabilities in existing senior managers, a strategy for disseminating the attributes throughout the organization, and a communications platform to help install and secure the forward momentum.

Outcomes of the G2 Defined Leadership Program:

1. Defined leadership capabilities and associated behaviors
2. Assessment of individual leaders and the executive team on the capabilities
3. Feedback of results and development of key actions to take the team and individuals forward
4. Defined capabilities to develop and evaluate future leaders

Using the 3C Organizational Performance Profile combined with Defined Leadership, organizations can raise their performance levels to higher levels very quickly.

Let's look at some examples. Perhaps you can relate or have experienced something similar to these at one time or another.

We once worked with an executive in charge of a large retail operation. When we were engaged, the company had just launched an organization-wide customer-service initiative. Our first meeting with the executive coincided with the unveiling of the program at the company headquarters. The scene was quite spectacular, with lobby displays, balloons, contests, and—the pinnacle in celebrations—a casual day. We were met in the lobby by our client, who was going to escort us to his office. We commented about the excitement happening all around us, and our client boasted about the importance of

3C© Performance Modeling

outstanding customer service in their competitive environment and how service would be a differentiating factor for them going forward. He certainly had his speaking points down and provided a convincing explanation for the effort and its associated costs. As he was sharing these comments with us, we entered an elevator that was crowded with a group of employees from the company's customer-assistance call center.

As the elevator climbed, another executive stepped on. We were introduced and learned he was in charge of merchandise returns. We learned this because the two executives debated the standing policy of requiring a register receipt when returning goods purchased at a store. A young woman, a customer-service representative from the call center, chimed in that one of the frequent complaints she heard daily was about this requirement. To her amazement, and to the shock of the others in the elevator, the leader of this organization noted that "most customers were out to rip them off" and that they "couldn't be trusted." He then went on for another 30 seconds about how certain "types of people" were always shoplifting and shouldn't be admitted to the stores. He said you could tell "who they were" because of how they talked and wore their clothes. We were dumbstruck. This was leadership modeling at its worst!

We had a similar experience at a company that had implemented a program designed to reduce operating costs by improving efficiencies and reducing waste. The sponsor of the program, our client, proudly introduced the initiative during an all-employee town-hall meeting and went on to explain how they could go on to the company's intranet and order a recommendation form that would be sent to them via interoffice mail. The form, a three-page carbon-copy design, was to be completed and then signed off on by the person's immediate boss. The person kept a copy, the boss kept a copy, and the remaining copy went to the task force set up to review ideas. When asked by an employee, "Why so many steps in the process?" and "Why a paper-based form?" the leader went on to share that, "Sometimes employees try to manipulate incentive programs by creating problems and inefficiencies and then offering solutions to the problems they made." He then concluded his talk by thanking them for their hard work and efforts. Here's an example of where leadership is trying to empower people (move them to competitive behavior) to identify waste, but modeling control behaviors by forcing the completion of forms — not to mention the trust issue (hardly connective)!

You can see that this type of behavior really derails the performance of an organization. Why should I be expected to perform the way the CEO is asking if my boss disagrees or if leadership is modeling a different behavior? We have seen this issue over and over again in organizations. Modeling comes with words and deeds. What leaders say and what they do speaks volumes. Nothing undermines organizational effort more than leadership behavior that is different or inconsistent; this provides room for misinterpretation and misunderstanding of acceptable behaviors.

This is why it is so critical that the leadership team is totally aligned regarding the type of Organizational Performance Profile they will communicate and models the behaviors they demand from the organization.

People need to know what is expected of them when they arrive at work each day. This is what creates excitement and commitment—their ability to meet expectations and deliver, to make a contribution to the success of the organization. Leaders must clearly define these expectations and ensure the organization is meeting those demands. This can be accomplished by using the Organizational Performance Profiling process outlined in Chapter 1. Additionally, leaders must align their leadership to the type of performance they need from the organization. They must model the behaviors and competencies that they expect their staff to deliver. This is what drives organizational performance.

CHAPTER 3

Individual Performance

We have discussed the importance of developing and communicating the required Organizational Performance Profile that leadership expects people to follow in the short term (people need to know how they are expected to act when they arrive at work). We have also shown the importance of modeling the appropriate leadership behaviors to support the profile and provide employees with a visible example of the expected behaviors.

What about individual preferences?

All of us—as individuals—have a preferred style of operating, and we usually work within that style, especially in stressful situations. These styles can also be described using the 3C language: compete, control, and connect. We have all three styles; however, one tends to be our area of comfort.

How do our preferred styles influence our daily work and therefore organizational performance?

Let's focus on a few "tools" that are used by organizations and managers to help employees perform their jobs. To keep things simple, we will focus on what we believe are the top three most commonly used tools: job descriptions, coaching, and personality testing.

We'll start with job descriptions.

It is common knowledge that organizations and leaders need to provide clarity on what is expected from individual employees. That is one of the main purposes of job descriptions:

47

to provide a clear definition of what is required for success on the job. Job descriptions are often updated annually but more often then not are updated when a specific job changes radically or a new job is created.

Job descriptions come in all sorts of shapes and sizes, but all provide some basic information, including:

- Title/name of position
- Key responsibilities
- Essential functions
- Required knowledge, skills, and abilities
- Required education and experience
- Any specific physical requirements

Our experience is that many organizations use job descriptions effectively—namely, to have an accurate depiction of job requirements in order to establish compensation levels and create performance metrics for use in performance evaluations. We find that job descriptions are typically used annually to formally review an individual's performance or to present a new position to an employee.

Most leaders, managers, and employees we have met view job descriptions as something required by HR and find the process of developing and/or using a job description tedious and sometimes unrelated to the business.

Job descriptions, like annual goals or vision statements, are really nothing more than a document describing the overall responsibilities of a particular position and the key skills required for success. But they do not outline what skills are needed when, nor do they state why those skills may be needed. Job descriptions, like annual goals, are "long term."

3C© Performance Modeling

They do not focus on what may be required today, what skills and behaviors must be employed to deliver what the boss requires right now.

Our observation is that employees need to know exactly what is required of them today—this week, right now. Knowing what is expected right now allows them to focus their energies specifically on that and to get it done more effectively. Now let's clarify something: we are not talking about providing step-by-step instructions on how to perform a job or what to do today. We are talking about the key outcomes the boss expects and/or needs in the short term. That allows employees to focus their efforts on those outcomes. It also forces the employee to use the correct skills to deliver those outcomes.

Let's take an example. Imagine yourself as a salesperson. Your job description has the standard "sales professional" tasks and responsibilities and states that you must demonstrate skills in establishing new prospects, sales calls, closing, etc. Maybe the key components look something like this:

- Maintaining and developing relationships with existing customers via meetings, telephone calls, and email
- Gathering market and customer information and entering into a customer tracking system
- Negotiating variations in price, delivery, and specifications with managers
- Advising on forthcoming product developments and discussing special promotions
- Checking quantities of goods on display in the showroom

- Recording sales and order information in CRMS and sending copies to the manager at the end of the day
- Reviewing own sales performance, aiming to meet or exceed targets
- Gaining a clear understanding of customers and requirements
- Making accurate, rapid cost calculations and providing customers with quotes

Let's also imagine that you have just joined the company and found that the sales department has gone through a complete restructuring. Further, there is a new sales-tracking system in place, and no one knows how to use it. Perhaps the first thing that is expected of you and the rest of the sales force is to learn the new system and ensure your customer and prospect data is properly entered into the system. That is the goal established by your boss for Week 1. Clearly, your focus will be on ensuring the data is properly recorded and accurate. Controlling behavior.

Toward the end of Week 1, your boss indicates that once you have CRMS fully updated, your focus needs to shift to outside calls. Now your focus shifts to competitive behaviors.

You are using different skill-sets at different periods of time.

A real-life example of this happened with one of our large clients. After being acquired, leadership focused on completely replacing the technology infrastructure associated with product tracking, customer tracking, and sales monitoring. It took three months to install the new system, train sales people on the system, and convert existing data. Additionally, policies and procedures needed to be redone. The decision made by leadership was to maintain a "minimum" level of customer calling—just enough to maintain positive relationships—while focusing most energies on the new system and training. After three months, once the system was implemented and sales people were fully trained, the focus shifted the execution: sales calls, new product introduction, growth. This is a classic example of an organization focusing on control and then moving to competition. Sales people understood the short-term focus, understood what was expected— and why—and understood that they would move back to aggressive sales calls within three months. It allowed people to bring different skills into play at the right time.

Another example concerns a real-estate client. After the housing bubble burst, the CEO switched the focus of his sales associates from competitive (getting listings and sales) to connective (building and maintaining existing relationships). His view was that these relationships would be critical when the market started turning, and he wanted his sales force focused on the right thing. Using Organizational Profiling, he was able to communicate this easily and effectively and have his agents shift to different behaviors almost overnight.

The message: it is critical for employees to know what is expected "today" and what will be expected "tomorrow" so they can employ the best skill-set to deliver.

Many organizations use personality profiles such as MBTI or DISC to help improve performance. The benefits of these tools can be substantive and include:

- Helping people better understand themselves, their strengths, and their own personal preferences
- Helping people better understand and appreciate individual differences in others and others' preferences

- Helping people learn to use their particular type to their own best advantage in dealing with others
- Helping people become more effective communicators by understanding personality types better
- Helping people improve their interpersonal communication
- Facilitating work-group functioning
- Enhancing individual performance in the workplace

Our experience using these tools has been excellent, and we believe they are very beneficial to personal growth and development and organizational performance. However, one of the dilemmas we have encountered is "stickiness." These tools tend to be complex, and often people forget over time how to best apply them. People tend to remember one aspect—their type—and may retain only a bit about styles other than theirs. Additionally, since they also involve a degree of personality testing, they tend to state, "This is who you are," implying that changing "who you are" can be difficult or perhaps impossible. We believe these tools are important contributors and have a major place in individual and organizational development. But they have a different purpose than what we are advocating in this book.

Our focus is on the ability of leaders to:

- Clearly define and communicate the organizational performance style for the short term
- Identify and model the leadership behaviors that reinforce the organizational behaviors necessary for success

- Encourage individuals and teams to shift their personal behavior to the required model

The key difference is one of flexibility; 3C does not state, "This is who you are." At an individual level, it merely shows your preference. Any individual has the ability to shift to different actions/behaviors to better meet organizational demands.

Our previous example of the real-estate firm exemplifies this. For years the sales associates were actively engaged in competitive behaviors—aggressively listing and selling homes. Once the new approach was clarified and leadership gave them permission (indeed, direction) to change, sales associates simply shifted to the highly relational connective style. Those who may have needed more help with this style received that support.

To initiate quick shifts like this, it is important to identify the behavior required (using the Organizational Performance Profile), and it is important for leadership to model the appropriate behavior (Defined Leadership). Additionally, it is important for individuals to shift their style.

We can use 3C to help with this. 3C is a way of looking at groups, leaders, and individuals in specific situations, at specific points in time. It is a short-term, repeatable program to direct planning and change to impact goal attainment. Using 3C, groups, organizations, and individuals are better able to focus their activities and efforts. In addition, 3C is a model to assess a team's readiness to deliver what is required for success. At the leadership level, 3C is a tool to assess and align leadership capabilities for specific short-term outcomes. Finally, 3C is a flexible tool to direct, change, and measure group and individual performance over time.

Our 3C model also applies to individuals:

A competitive focus:

- The drive for results and execution
- A focus on delivering expected outcomes quickly
- An opportunistic, energetic, intense, focused, targeted, driven, risk-taking, and goal-oriented organization

A controlling focus:

- A preference for process
- A focus on structure, order, and methodology
- A logical, analytical, and metric-focused organization

A connective focus:

- A drive for involvement and interaction
- A focus on relationships—how the pieces all fit and work together
- An organization focused on working together, having a broad outlook and perspective, inclusive activities

Individuals all have all three, but, as previously stated, we each have a preferred discipline or style. We prefer to operate in our preferred style, and we certainly operate in this style when we are under stress.

To attain annual or even long-term goals, organizations, teams, and individuals are constantly adapting, making slight (or major) changes in operational direction as different situations demand. To get from point A to point B is *never* a straight line; it is a series of turns, ultimately arriving at the destination. These turns mean that the organization needs different styles at each turn. For example, an organization or team may find that implementation of a new system or product requires an unanticipated change in the policy and procedures required to deliver that product, forcing the team to focus on developing those procedures before going to market. Individuals need to adapt their styles and behaviors to more closely align with what the organization is demanding.

3C is about behaviors—and behaviors can be chosen. It is important to reemphasize that we have all three skill-sets within us (controlling behaviors, competitive behaviors, and connective behaviors). Unlike many personality tools and assessments, 3C does not limit us. We can—*and do*—act in ways that are competitive, controlling, and connective. We have all three disciplines and use traits associated with all three numerous times during the day. We change our behaviors based on our needs.

Everyone has a preferred style. Let's review the traits and behaviors associated with each style.

Competitors

Competitors see a world of many choices, some facts, and some connections. This means that they see a world of action filled with many opportunities, challenges to overcome, and goals to attain. Goal attainment is critically important to competitors, and they build actions around it. The world may be complicated, but they see it as simple and straightforward and identify quick solutions. They are focused, disciplined, and demanding in making choices. Competitors value action, strength, and responsibility. They may not notice other issues, other possibilities, or other people as they focus primarily on accomplishing the goal.

Some common descriptions of competitors include:

strong, demanding, certain, commanding, driven, impatient, blunt

Personal Characteristics
Attributes associated with the competitor profile include:

- Strong
- Determined
- Judgmental
- Focused
- Assured
- Tough
- Opinionated
- Adventurous
- Bold
- Intense

Communication Style
Attributes associated with the competitor profile include:

- Outspoken
- Abrupt
- Uses slogans
- Urgent and quick
- Grand gestures
- Impromptu
- Impulsive
- Clear and simple
- Candid
- Brief

Work Style
Attributes associated with the competitor profile include:

- High impact / speed
- inspires people
- Outspoken
- Risk taking
- Engages & Commits
- Loves pressure (creates it)
- Demands clarity
- Disciplined
- Unambiguous
- Results-driven

3C© Performance Modeling

Controllers

Controllers focus on facts and analytics, with some choices and complexity. Careful analysis and planning almost always precedes action—it is better to measure twice and cut once. Their world is structured and reasonable and is influenced and shaped by facts, logic, time limits, and the best approach to each situation. Improvising is difficult for controllers. Drama, emotion, and impulse action are distracting. Their talent is discovering methods, systems, and techniques for making things work well. Controllers set high standards and seek mastery and perfection in all their efforts

Some common descriptions of controllers include:

rational, diplomatic, objective, methodical, precise, prepared, practical

Personal Characteristics

Attributes associated with the controller profile include:

- Rational
- Analytical
- Acquisitive
- Industrious
- Grand gestures
- Systematic
- Reflective
- Reserved
- Insightful
- Articulate
- Precise
- Cautious

Communication Style

Attributes associated with the controller profile include:

- Logical
- Cool/detached
- Matter of fact
- Literal
- Prepared
- Controlled

- Disengaged
- Systematic
- Patient
- Cautious

Work Style

Attributes associated with the controller profile include:

- Organized
- Methodical
- Thorough
- Cautious
- Measured
- Orderly, efficient
- Calm
- Professional
- Cooperative
- Perfectionist

Connectors

A connector's world is complex and holistic with many, many choices and limited structure. They see the world like a medley of colors, events, or interactions, with ever-changing patterns among people, events, and ideas. They see the many interactions and relationships in their surroundings. Connectors respond to shading and nuance and distrust rigid categories and simplistic rules. They are most comfortable in less-structured situations. Connectors learn by participating and interacting. They tell stories and generate images to capture the rapid flow of ideas around them. They have high energy and a high need to engage and include others. It is often difficult for others to understand them because they do not see all the connections connectors see.

Some common descriptions of connectors include:
expressive, spontaneous, intuitive, involved, engaging, unpredictable, energetic

Personal Characteristics

Attributes associated with the connector profile include:

3C© Performance Modeling

- Warm and open
- Trusting
- Perceptive
- Sympathetic
- Accepting

- Intuitive
- Engaged
- Fun-loving
- Flexible
- Spontaneous

Communication Style
Attributes associated with the connector profile include:

- Inclusive
- Sensitive
- Relational
- Uses metaphors
- Expressive

- Responsive
- Calm
- Nonjudgmental
- Dramatic
- Performing

Work Style
Attributes associated with the connector profile include:

- Facilitator
- Team Player
- Attentive listener
- Collaborative
- Energetic

- Networker
- Harmonizer
- Creative
- Experimental
- Open (invites input)

As you can see, the styles differ greatly. As we have stated, everyone can easily operate in any of the styles, but each of us has a preferred style, and our desire is to remain in that style and interact with people in that style. It is our comfort zone.

Once leadership has clearly defined the organization style/behaviors required for the short term, the individual has a responsibility to bring those behaviors into action. In many cases, this will mean moving out of their preferred style. In order to best accomplish this, individuals need to know their preferred styles so they can more easily move to the style required as well as understand some of the issues they may face while making the change. Again, we are not saying the other two styles disappear; it is more of a rebalancing.

We can compare the preferred style of an individual to the desired profile of the organization set by leadership:

Desired Profile

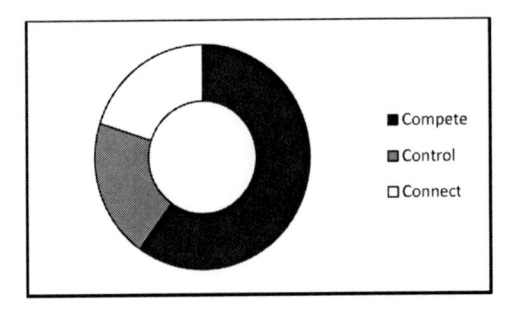

[Donut chart showing Compete, Control, Connect]

Individual Profile

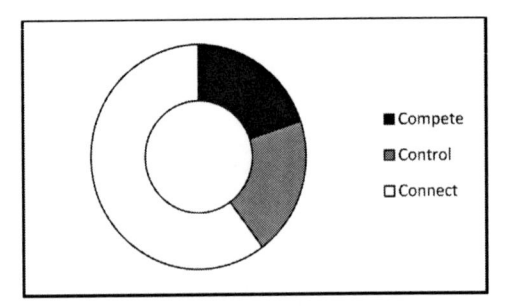

[Donut chart showing Compete, Control, Connect]

We can clearly see that the individual prefers a connected style of work, but the organization is calling for a more competitive style. This individual knows she will have to rebalance her approach to focus more on the competitive skills outlined above. She will have to move to execution

3C© Performance Modeling

and delivery, moving away from her preference of high involvement and interaction and a concern for how everything fits together. She needs to deliver—now.

Some will find it a bit difficult moving away from their preferred style. However, our experience shows that once people know what is expected of them, the shift is easier. Further, once they know and understand what difficulties they may encounter, the shift is easier.

We can summarize the potential difficulty individuals may have in changing focus as follows:

Persons with a Less Preferred Competitive Drive

Individuals whose nature is not competitive tend to be more cautious and reserved than others. Though equally focused on achieving results, their actions and behaviors are more grounded in process, data, circumstances, and implications. "Soft" competitive-drive individuals take careful aim, then fire. For them, getting the right results means taking the appropriate time to ensure all efforts are fruitful. The trade-off is accuracy and completion versus speed.

Persons with a Less Preferred Controlling Drive

Individuals whose nature is not controlling tend to be more spontaneous and impulsive than others. For these individuals, structure tends to impede creativity and outcomes. These persons like to experiment and are quite comfortable with little to no guidance or direction. Though focused on quality, their actions and behaviors are more grounded in action and consequences. "Soft" competitive-drive individuals pick up the gun and pull the trigger without checking for ammunition or seeing if the safety lock is engaged. For them, getting the right results means experimenting, breaking traditions to ensure all efforts are fruitful. The trade-off is speed versus structure, process and repeatability/replication.

Persons with a Less Preferred Connective Drive

Individuals whose nature is not connective tend to be more concrete and objective in their approach. Subjectivity, "gut" feelings, or intuition are not natural for them. The latest gossip and/or office rumors are more an inconvenience and nuisance than a form of information or recreation. These individuals are not good with subtlety; they prefer to be told the cold, hard facts and tend to express their opinions in kind. "Soft" connective persons tend to see things in absolutes—things are black and white—and are more comfortable when events or actions are presented in a simplistic, logical order. Though able to focus on the interconnectivity of people, events, and consequences, their comfort zone is more about individual events or actions. "Soft" competitive-drive individuals pick up the gun and pull the trigger. The trade-off here is action and results versus longer-term consequences and implications, team involvement, and inclusion.

As you can see, this allows individuals and leadership to focus on those areas that may warrant additional training or support to ensure that performance is accelerated.

The 3C Performance Profiling System accelerates performance to higher levels. It is a simple tool that provides a common language for performance improvement.

Focusing on three levels—the organization/team, leadership, and individuals—it provides a quick and easy way to navigate the path to superior results.

3C Performance Profiling

The Path to Results

The Organizational Profile

- Leadership defines the required organizational Performance Profile for short-term focus
- The team then defines the "actual profile"—how the company is currently working
- The required profile is reviewed, defined, and implemented

The Leadership Profile

- Defines leadership attributes and behaviors for success for required organizational profile

The Individual Profile

- Defines an individual's comfort profile—how he or she likes to perform work

It becomes clear that once leadership has defined the Performance Profile required for the next two to three months (and agree on that profile), and once leadership and the organization understand the requirements of the profile, and once individuals know what is expected of them, the process of moving to the new profile moves to the forefront. Individuals and teams can identify the blockers to moving to the new profile, and leadership can resolve them, thus accelerating change.

CHAPTER 4

Team Performance

Most work is done by teams. There are reasons for this. A team encourages people to divide work into functional components and to develop levels of specialization, skills, and knowledge in dealing with each of these components, leading to a level of performance rarely attainable by an individual. A team of ten people can usually greatly outperform 10 individuals working separately.

Most persons have had experience being a part of a team. And while most examples used in "team" discussions tend to be taken from the world of sports, there are in fact many different kinds of teams. Consider the following:

- **A Surgical Team:** Highly specialized skills with specific and unique responsibilities and roles. Little if any exchange of duties.

- **An Orchestra:** Specific talents that, when blended, create harmony. Some musicians may be able to play different instruments; however, they have a primary place in the orchestra and specific music to play.

- **A Fire Brigade:** Highly practiced roles that complement and augment one another. Firefighters are cross-trained to be familiar with any piece of equipment required to subdue a fire.

Even within the realm of sports there are very different types of teams. For example:

- **Track and Field:** Specialists, such as a pole vaulter. An individual athlete can succeed, and yet the team can lose.

- **Doubles in Tennis:** Both players are active and involved in all plays, though only one player can hit the ball.

- **Baseball:** In baseball, most players for the team in the field are inactive during play. Unless there is a hit, only the pitcher, catcher, and batter are actively involved. Rarely are there plays where more than 1/3 of the players on the field for a team are participating. For the team at bat, only one person can hit at a time, and unless there are base runners, eight of the nine players are sitting and watching the action.

- **Crew:** All of the rowers in a crew scull must not only pull in the same direction but at the same time as well—rhythm and unison are keys to success.

The point is there are many types of teams. While there are commonalities we can outline, the differences are important. The level of specialization and interdependence varies based on the type of team. In the business setting, teams can take different forms as well. There are intact work teams (such as the payroll department), cross-functional work teams (for example, a task force established to implement a new technology platform), and ad-hoc teams (such as a group brought together for the one-time purpose of brainstorming a solution to a current operating problem). Finally, there are informal teams, such as a group of employees looking to coordinate a fund-raising event for the community or the holiday party for the department.

Understanding the type of team you are a part of is a critical first step. If there is a high level of specialization and a great deal of interdependency, there are specific areas to focus on. The more a team relies upon the unique skills and abilities of a subject-matter expert, the greater the risk of a failure due to the interdependence. In the example of a surgical team, each person has a specific role to play, and although there is essential collaboration, if the patient dies because the anesthetist overmedicated him, the team failed. If the bass-drum section (or even one drummer) in an orchestra is off tempo, the musical performance could be dismal. Specialization is a blessing and a curse. Specialization tied to highly interdependent functions can be a recipe for success— or sometimes failure.

For example, imagine you and nine other people each work independently of each other on a job that requires you to receive phone calls from customers requesting information, supply that information, and enter details about the call into your computer. Imagine also that computer problems sometimes disrupt this work. If you are working independently, all of you will need to learn to diagnose and service your machines, losing customer-contact time. As a team, however, you could decide to make one person a specialist in computer diagnosis and servicing. Whenever you have problems, you call this person over, and you use another computer until yours is ready. And perhaps each person specializes in specific types of products or information and has calls routed (by a voice-response unit, a computer, or another specialist) when a customer needs information in which you are an expert. This would also begin to improve performance.

But there is more to it than economic efficiency. When

psychologists began studying work teams many years ago, they were surprised to discover how important teams were to the lives of the people on them. People are social creatures, and teams are social systems. People who enjoy their teams, who have friends on their teams, enjoy their work. People who feel excluded and like outsiders do not enjoy their work.

Different types of work are best accomplished by different types of teams. Teams differ in their typical missions, in their typical roles, and in their typical norms. The result is that teams perform very differently, and these differences make the teams effective for different kinds of tasks and responsibilities.

Our model here is very simple; we are going to suggest that there are three macro types of teams: teams that focus on action missions, teams that focus on process missions, and teams that focus on content missions. None of these types are better than any other type; they are simply different. Each of these types of teams can accomplish tasks easily that are difficult for the others, but no one type of team can do everything.

We can link these three team types to the three Cs of performance.

- Competitor-Oriented: Teams are action-oriented— oriented toward actions outside the team itself.

- Control-Oriented: Teams are process-oriented— oriented toward methodology and process, the steps necessary for completion.

- Connect-Oriented: Teams are content-oriented— oriented toward the internal maintenance tasks and their impact on other areas and how everything fits together.

3C© Performance Modeling

This model is deliberately simplified. All teams perform action functions, content functions, and process functions. However, different teams emphasize different functions.

Calling a team a competitor-oriented team, a control-oriented team, or a connect-oriented team simply identifies its *primary focus*. It also provides clarity to team members regarding the expected behaviors and approach required. Knowing their individual performance preference (as outlined in Chapter 3), team members can shift (if necessary) to emphasize the required behaviors and approach.

When individual team members remain in their preferred style, differences occur, communication breaks down and, ultimately, performance of the team suffers.

It is the responsibility of leadership to clearly define the expectations!

Imagine a team composed mostly of connectors, and leadership expects a fast result. Without defining that leadership needs competitor behavior, the team will spend an inordinate amount of time building relationships and history… and may not deliver on time.

Imagine a team of mostly competitor types tasked with developing a review process to prevent fraud. Without direction to "move to control," they will complete it in one hour, and it will probably be missing key steps. They will be focused on getting it done rather than getting it done correctly.

Finally, imagine a team of controllers tasked with speeding up a loan-approval process. Well, you get the drill. Clarifying expectations and type of team performance that is required is critical.

Let's review the makeup of the different types of teams.

Competitor-Oriented Teams: Action Orientation

Competitor-oriented teams are action teams, collections of individuals united around shared goals. The primary responsibility of the leadership of these teams is to provide the sense of shared goals around which the team acts. The primary responsibility of the membership is to enroll their talents around these goals.

The primary roles are:

- Results
- Energizer
- Confronter
- Promoter
- Director
- Advocate

Competitor-oriented teams are especially suited for missions that require facing the world outside the team, the capacity for rapid response to the world based on limited information, and the confidence to believe that the world can be shaped by the team.

Control-Oriented Teams: Process Orientation

These are process teams, collections of experts united around process or methodologies, using knowledge and process to solve concrete problems. The primary responsibility of leadership in these teams is to focus and coordinate these common interests to achieve mastery of specific problems; the primary responsibility of members is to enroll their specific expertise in the service of the team goals.

The primary roles are:
- Process/methodology
- Information seeker
- Tracker
- Tester
- Regulator

Members evaluate each other largely in terms of their professional qualifications and performances. The model for these teams is the seminar, laboratory, or motor pool. Control-oriented teams are especially suited to missions that require expertise, specialization of knowledge and skills, and the ability to organize complex resources to serve specific ends.

Connect-Oriented Teams: Content Orientation

These are relational teams, oriented primarily to their own internal dynamics and to the global impact their efforts will have on the organization. A connect-oriented team is molded by its common history and by its concern for the intricate processes of integrating this specific group of people with the specific tasks which need to be accomplished.

The primary responsibility of the leadership is sensitivity to the needs of the team; the primary responsibility of membership is sensitivity to the team identity.

The primary roles are:
- Coordinator
- Harmonizer
- Supporter
- Facilitator

Connect-oriented teams tend to be tremendously stable; they devote enormous energy to the maintenance of the team, and the result is an enduring, consistently productive work team. These teams are also capable of absorbing large numbers of members; these are potentially the largest teams. The process of inclusion is important to these teams. People who are drawn to these teams typically have excellent and natural team skills. The model for these teams is the family or neighborhood.

Connect-oriented teams are especially suited to missions that require stability and consistency of response, that require long-term relationships and patterns of interaction, and that require sensitivity to complex patterns of interaction within the team and between the team and the rest of the world.

Team Makeup

All work teams need to perform all three of the key group functions of action, content, and relationships. Different types of teams may give different emphases to these functions; however, no successful group can ignore any of these three functions.

Teams can and should use people of varied preferences to help the team fulfill its mission. Teams cannot, however, allow the varied interests, values, and concerns of its varied members to subvert the mission of the team. It is the responsibility of the leadership of the team to define the performance required from the team and for team members to employ that style (not at the exclusion of other styles but certainly a rebalance). This requires that the leaders understand both their members and their mission.

3C© Performance Modeling

Effective team performance first requires an identification of the type of outcome and the approach needed to best attain that outcome (compete, control, or connect). Once that is clear, team members can rebalance their approach to meet the team mission. They can also use other *C* attributes to ensure that the team does not get out of balance.

Using the 3C modeling for team performance will ultimately improve team effectiveness.

CHAPTER 5

Mergers and Acquisitions

Companies that acquire other organizations or merge with other organizations typically face a tough "post-merger/acquisition period" when both organizations are trying to align their operations. This period can be quite traumatic and have a negative impact on performance, as employees look to find their way in the new organization, search for an understanding of the new expectations, and—sometimes—wait for leadership to set the directions. A key leadership challenge, therefore, is to accelerate this transition by addressing the problems before they arise.

Dealing with a merger or acquisition greatly impacts a leader's time and management focus. Too often, potential difficulties seem trivial to managers caught up in the thrill of the big deal. However, these difficulties can and do derail momentum and often result in lower than expected results. The chances for success are further hampered if the two organizations have different corporate cultures. Acquisition or mergers are typically based on potential operational or market synergies: operational efficiencies, grabbing additional market share, or adding product or technology capabilities. All too often, the organizational performance/operating style differences are ignored. It's a mistake to assume that personnel issues are easily overcome. These aspects of a working environment are significant, and failure to address them before, during, and after the merger/acquisition can result in failure.

Studies show that close to two-thirds of organizational transitions fail because management spends time on the deal instead of focusing on the post-merger environment required to make the new organization productive. Focus on how the organization works and how the new organization is expected to work is critical to success.

Managers and employees need to know the basics:

- *What* is happening?
- *Why* is it happening—what are the compelling reasons and drivers of this change?
- *How* are they expected to perform—how should they operate in this new environment?
- WIFM—what's in it for me?

We continue to present this simple model because it works. It is even more important for leadership to address these issues before and immediately after the organizational merger/acquisition. The *what* and the *why* are the responsibility of leadership. It's not a democratic process, so this is simply a matter of clear communication. *How* is a joint responsibility; leadership and management must clearly define how they expect the organization to operate, and the organization must have the opportunity to define what is getting in the way and what they need to deliver what is required.

The Organizational Performance Profile and related Defined Leadership approach can help accelerate transition to the desired state. As a matter of fact, it is helpful to use the profile prior to the acquisition/merger to get a better understanding of the differences between how the two organizations are operating and to help identify the issues the leadership team must confront. Getting a head start on these key organizational issues makes the transition easier because both organizations are aware of the new desired state. This works well with mergers and acquisitions as well as when combining teams or departments. A lot of post-merger time can be saved and performance can be accelerated by ensuring these issues are identified and effectively managed.

Let's take an example. Suppose Company A is acquiring Company B. Both are in the same industry, and it is pretty clear that the acquisition will provide Company A with more clients, a better technology platform, and entry into a new geographic market. Further, let's say Company A is a large Fortune 500 company with good performance, seasoned leadership, and well-established policies and procedures. If we ran the Organizational Performance Profile for Company A, it would be fairly balanced, with a leaning toward the connective discipline:

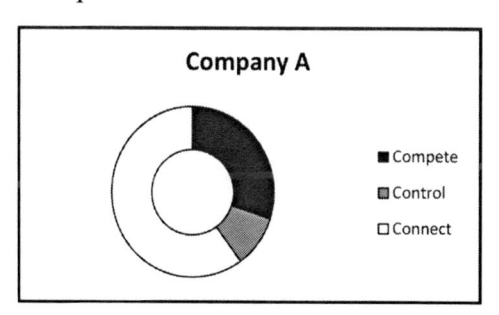

Company A

■ Compete
▨ Control
☐ Connect

Leadership is focused on cross-functional/department integration and utilization, cross-sales, etc. We can summarize the profile and leadership styles like this:

Organizational Performance Expectations

A focus on the interactive nature of work, high involvement, relationship, and a collective effort. A systemic and holistic orientation, concerned with how things "fit" or do not "fit" together.

Core Competencies of a Connective-Oriented Leader

- Imaginative—can see many opportunities and relationships
- Highly diplomatic
- Generates ideas for others
- Relationship builder
- Champions harmony and consistency toward goals
- Collaborative
- Values diversity and different perspectives

Company B is a smaller company and has been focused on revenue growth for the past four years, expanding rapidly. Running the Organizational Performance Profile for this company would show a high focus on the competitive discipline, moderate to low focus on the control, and a low focus on the connective discipline.

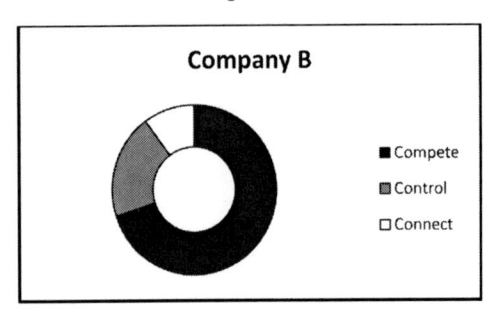

Company B

- Compete
- Control
- Connect

3C© Performance Modeling

This profile and related leadership styles would look like this:

Organizational Performance Expectations

A focused, targeted, driven, risk-taking, goal-oriented, and persevering organization focused on results and delivery.

Core Competencies of a Competitive-Oriented Leader
- Sets clear, bold goals
- Drives change; seeks opportunities
- Visionary
- Drives performance and execution
- Maintains motivating pressure on businesses and people
- Delivers results
- High risk tolerance

You can immediately see the inconsistencies in both organizational expectations and leadership style.

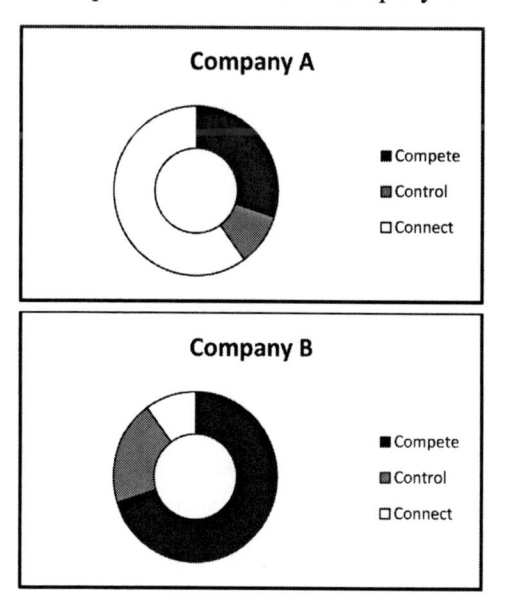

Company A

- Compete
- Control
- Connect

Company B

- Compete
- Control
- Connect

Company B will have a difficult time "slowing down" and assuming the more holistic style of Company A both at the leadership level and throughout the organization.

Staff in Company B will be anxious to learn what is expected of them. Once they know and understand that, they can then begin participating in the post acquisition activities to ensure a smooth transition—namely, changing their work programs and ensuring management knows the blockers that may hinder their success.

The good news is that by using the profile to identify these differences ahead of time, leadership has the ability to identify and communicate the desired state to the entire organization of Company B, allowing people to 1) know and understand what is expected going forward, 2) identify what is needed to transition to the new state, and 3) develop action plans to accelerate the transition.

In this case, the leadership of Company A has an initial decision to make; namely, whether they want Company B to continue with its existing Performance Profile—competitive, focused on execution and results with a high risk tolerance—or whether they want Company B to begin transitioning to the profile currently in place at Company A. It is absolutely critical that leadership makes this decision, communicates, and allows Company B to operate. Once this decision is made and the required profile is clear and understood, leadership and management can begin executing the post-acquisition goals quickly and efficiently.

Earlier in this book we shared one of our foundational models regarding performance. It begs repeating here. People fail to perform for one of four reasons:

A. They don't know what they are supposed to do

B. They know what they are suppose to do but don't know how to do it

C. They are aware of what they should do, know how to do it, but cannot due to process and/or policy constraints

D. They know what they are supposed to do, know how to do it, and have no obstacle facing them, but they just don't want to do it

Using the Performance Profile, we have clearly addressed A, B, and C: there is clarity on what they are supposed to do, they have the responsibility of identifying (for management) the policies and processes getting in the way, and they have been trained as required. If D exists, then it is a performance-management issue.

Using the associated leadership behaviors, we can communicate to leaders of both organizations the types of behaviors to model and how they will have to adjust to make the integration as positive and quick as possible.

This can and should be an integral part of the post-merger/acquisition plan. Additionally, the acquiring company can better evaluate the leadership team and determine the best lineup for quick transition.

All too often, consultants have been brought in to help resolve post-acquisition organizational issues, almost all of which could be identified ahead of time.

A real example of these types of "profile mismatches" occurred while we were working with a client who had acquired a smaller, more nimble regional competitor, similar to our example above. Our client, a large and well-established leader in its industry, had recently completed an 18-month quality-improvement initiative using a Six Sigma process.

Through those efforts, our client restructured a number of internal operating procedures and significantly enhanced oversight and review processes to improve quality. Our client was focused on control. The acquired company was more of an industry maverick—with creative marketing, sales, and delivery methods. Those methods enabled them to expand their market share quickly in a highly competitive geographic region. The acquired company had sales-incentive programs and a robust cross-selling practice. The acquired company was clearly focused on *compete*. Through the use of the Performance Profile, these differences were highlighted and effectively engaged at the executive level.

The organizational profiles looked something like this:

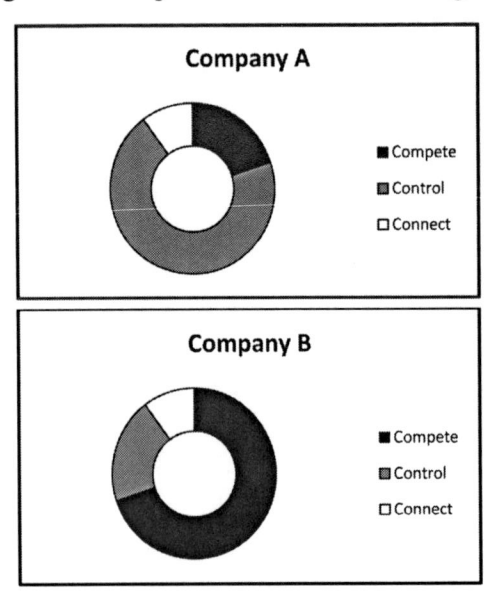

Company A

- Compete
- Control
- Connect

Company B

- Compete
- Control
- Connect

In another engagement, the "culture clash" was more disruptive. We were brought in post-integration and faced two very different business perspectives. Our client in this case

3C© Performance Modeling

was a family owned and operated business that grew from one retail location to over 30, mostly in smaller communities. Through all of that expansion, the core values of the company—family, quality, and customer convenience—were carefully molded and embedded in each new store. For our client, the focus was on connection and control. In a bid to leap-frog their closest competitor, the management team (all founding family members) acquired a struggling regional retail chain that was based in and operated throughout the busy Baltimore/Washington corridor. This organization was very different not only in their customer base (mostly suburban versus rural) but also in their business philosophy—offering lower-priced, less expensive goods and betting on sales volume. The employees tended to focus more on bigger-ticket products (such as electronics) because they were paid a sales commission. For this company, the focus was on *compete*. As the acquired company struggled financially, they laid off sales staff, which affected customer service. Again, having the leadership team outline their expectations via the Performance Profile, we were able to quickly and easily outline management's focus and direction for the organization.

The organizational profiles looked like this:

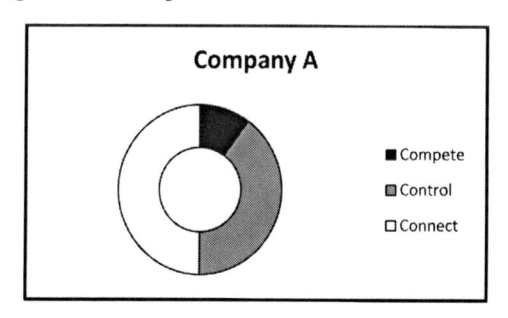

Company A

- ■ Compete
- ▣ Control
- ☐ Connect

Company B

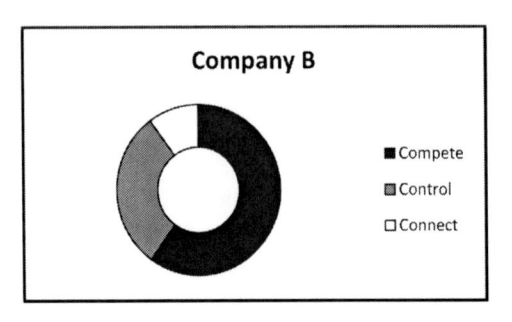

- Compete
- Control
- Connect

    The leadership profiles of the organizations, of course, were vastly different also, creating problems in setting priorities and moving forward. As you can see, there is ample opportunity for problems to arise. The key, however, is awareness. As long as leadership is aware of the potential problems, they can be addressed and resolved. This allows for a quicker transition to the new state and improved organizational performance.

    One of the key variables in any successful merger and/or acquisition is leadership. Executives from both organizations must:

- Understand the current operating profile of both companies
- Clarify the desired operating profile of both companies
- Clarify the "final" operating profile
- Hold leadership accountable for the correct modeling of behaviors

    Once leadership and the organizations understand what is expected, transition action planning can begin and will be effective.

    Using Organizational and Leadership Performance Profiling before and during a merger or acquisition can help smooth the process and accelerate transition to recognizing

3C© Performance Modeling

synergies. Building simple awareness of the desired state and the leadership styles required to attain that state will speed the process.

ABOUT THE AUTHORS

Glenn Schenenga

Glenn began his professional career with Citibank in the mid-1970s after five years as a pilot in the US Navy. Holding various positions in operations management and human resources within the commercial, investment, and retail banking organizations of Citibank, Glenn moved to director of human resources and training for the investment-banking arm of the organization in the late 1980s. He then served as director of acquisitions integration for the retail bank during a period of rapid expansion/acquisition. In early 1990, Glenn moved to consulting, focusing on executive team dynamics, change management, and executive coaching. In addition, he owned and operated a small technology training business. He holds an MBA from Fairleigh Dickinson University.

Gregory Gamble

Greg has worked as a trainer, facilitator, internal consultant, and human resources director in a number of industries. For close to 20 years he has focused on helping organizations achieve their business objectives and individuals achieve personal and professional goals. He has extensive experience with team dynamics, performance-improvement efforts, and organizational change initiatives. He holds an MA from Indiana State University and an undergraduate degree from Marietta College.

For more information on 3C Performance Modeling, contact us at: **info@g2ptnrs.com** or **www.g2ptnrs.com**.